HEART
of a
BIRTHMOM

HEART
of a
BIRTHMOM

A DEVOTIONAL GUIDE *for* BIRTHMOTHERS

TERRI GAKE, M.S.

WinePressPublishing
Great Books, Defined.

WinePress Publishing (PO Box 428, Enumclaw, WA 98022) functions only as book publisher. As such, the ultimate design, content, editorial accuracy, and views expressed or implied in this work are those of the author.

ISBN 13: 978-1-4141-1963-2
ISBN 10: 1-4141-1963-1
Library of Congress Catalog Card Number: 2010939288

To Mark, who has given my heart an earthly home.
To Jesus, who has given me an eternal one.

ABRAHAM, ISAAC, AND ME

God said, "Abraham!" "Yes?" answered Abraham. "I'm listening." He said, "Take your dear son Isaac whom you love and go to the land of Moriah. Sacrifice him there as a burnt offering on one of the mountains that I'll point out to you."...Abraham told his two young servants, "Stay here with the donkey. The boy and I are going over there to worship; then we'll come back to you."

—Genesis 22:1-5

AS A BIRTH mother, this is the passage of the Bible I have always claimed as my own. Who else on earth can better understand what Abraham was feeling than a birth mother? We have been at that place and have chosen a different life for our children regardless of the consequences. To this day, I get emotional thinking about what God asked Abraham to do. I am awed by the faith Abraham had in order to follow God's direction to the letter.

Notice what Abraham says to the servants. He says that he and the boy are going to worship and then "*we* will come back." God had asked him to sacrifice his one and only son, yet Abraham's faith was so big that he was sure his son would be returning with him.

When I signed those papers and released my daughter into the care of another, it felt like this passage feels. I had no promise that I would ever see her again. I had no idea what the days ahead would hold. I just did it. In the same way, the Bible says nothing of Abraham's state

1

of mind. We don't hear him complaining. We don't even see him hesitating. What we see is Abraham snapping to attention and doing exactly what God asked of him. God doesn't intervene until that last possible moment. God wanted to know if Abraham was really going to follow through. The Bible says "…he reached out his hand and took the knife to slay his son." That is when God stopped him—at the last possible moment.

It's interesting that God chooses Abraham for this task instead of Isaac's mother. Obviously, God is preparing him for a higher calling. As a result of meeting this challenge with obedience, God promises to make Abraham's descendants as numerous as the stars in the sky and as the sand on the seashore. This is a promise that God fulfills throughout the rest of the Bible.

Are you willing to trust God no matter what he asks you to do? Are you willing to follow him despite obstacles and difficulties? Take a minute and reflect on your relationship with God.

A TIME FOR EVERYTHING

There's an opportune time to do things, a right time for everything on the earth:…A right time to cry and another to laugh, a right time to lament and another to cheer…

—Ecclesiastes 3:1,8

D ID YOU KNOW that the loss of a child is near the top of the list of most traumatic life events? Actually, it is number four, under "death of a close family member." I know you're thinking *but my child isn't dead.* Consider this, though. Adoption is a type of loss. Just like a miscarriage. Just like abortion. I know that sounds terrible, but think about it for a minute. The child you have grown attached to and loved and carried to term—only to give to someone else—is gone. Even though you may have regular contact with that child and their family, you are no longer the parent. You don't have decision-making power over the child anymore.

This is what you are experiencing right now, wherever you are in your journey. You have lost a child not to death or divorce, but to adoption. Although you made the best decision as a parent, given the circumstances, this is still a loss for you. Give yourself some grace if you find yourself not bouncing back right away. Things are never going to be the same as before. I know you may be waiting for life to get back to "normal," but it never will. You are in the process of establishing a new "normal." I wish I could tell you what it's supposed to look like, but no one knows.

Shortly after my daughter was born, my family moved. In reading my old journals, I was looking for what got me through those first days, weeks, and months. Time is so linear it just keeps on going no matter what. That can be reassuring and frustrating all at the same time. What I found was that life kept me going. Getting up, working, going to school, having friends, having family…that's what kept me going. Those days were long and seemingly endless. I cried night after night. The hole in my heart was still raw and very real. But just like we have to get back on a bicycle after falling off, I had to keep living. I had to keep putting one foot in front of the other. Sure, I would have good days and depressing days, but I kept going.

The hard part for you may be *how* to keep going. Maybe your whole life has been uprooted by your pregnancy. I don't know what your circumstances are. What I can encourage you to do is to make right choices as you are establishing your new "normal." These are foundational choices you are making, no matter what your age and stage in life. Find a church in your area that offers a support group or a Bible study that interests you. Find a counselor in your area that specializes in grief. Lean on friends and family members who really want to be there for you. They may not understand what you are going through, but let them help you. Tell them how you feel. Ask them for help. They love you and want to help you; they just may not know how.

Take a minute and write in your journal. Has this been a good day? An average day? A hard day? Think about what contributed to the kind of day you have had. Being able to identify the things that make you take a nose dive is one step in regaining control over your life.

TAKING GOD AT HIS WORD

> Then we set out from Horeb and headed for the Amorite hill country, going through that huge and frightening wilderness that you've had more than an eyeful of by now…There I told you, "You've made it to the Amorite hill country that GOD, our God, is giving us. Look, GOD…has placed this land as a gift before you. Go ahead and take it now. GOD…promised it to you. Don't be afraid. Don't lose heart."
> —Deuteronomy 1:19-21

THE SLAVES THAT used to live in Egypt had been freed. God had done miraculous things to free them from a mean-spirited Pharaoh. He took them to a new place, literally a new country, where they could live and worship God however they wanted. They would truly be free. God had promised it.

But when they got to this "promised land," they saw giant people and were afraid. Instead of reaching the Promised Land in the short time God had told them it would take, these people took forty years to arrive. Why? Because they didn't trust God at his word.

They finally arrived, but God was so angry at this group of people for not believing him that he waited until an entire generation died out before letting them into their promised country.

We can do things our way, or we can do things God's way. Now, God's way doesn't always make sense to us. In fact, in my life it rarely makes sense. In my limited vision, I can only see what is in front of me.

But God sees the whole picture. He sees the end from the beginning. We don't see it because we are only on this earth for a blip of time. God is eternal. If we are truly going to trust him and follow him, we have to be willing to do things his way. Even when it doesn't make sense. *Especially when it doesn't make sense.* Our faith is our beliefs put into action. We do that by trusting God more than we trust ourselves and our limited vision.

Take a minute now and write in your journal. What's going on in your life right now that requires you to trust God? Is he telling you to do something that doesn't make sense to you? Pray right now for the courage and faith to follow him even when it seems crazy.

ATTITUDE ADJUSTMENT

> I don't know about you, but I'm running hard for the finish line. I'm giving it everything I've got. No sloppy living for me! I'm staying alert and in top condition. I'm not going to get caught napping…
> —1 Corinthians 9:26-27

I LOVE WORKING out. I'm a jazzerciser, actually. I love it so much. The loud music, the dancing, the camaraderie…it's my own little piece of paradise in the world. I get up and leave the house before anyone else gets up, just so I can enjoy a few minutes to myself at the start of each day. Every day for one hour, I tune out the worries and the pressures in my life so that all that matters is the next step or song.

Although I have to make myself take a day off, I don't always feel very peppy. Some days I wake up before my alarm goes off. Other days I hit the snooze button once or twice. Some days I can do high impact, but on other days I have to take it down a notch. The reason I keep going is the end result. I know in the end I will feel better, look better, sleep better, and have a better attitude with those around me. I don't always feel like working out, but I go anyway.

Working out when I don't feel like it is taking mastery over my feelings. You are in control of you, no matter how you *feel*. You will have up days and down days. That's normal. But instead of making decisions based on how you feel, make decisions based on the big picture. Where do you want to be in five years, ten years? Physical fitness is important.

So are other considerations like: What kind of job do you want to have? What kind of student do you want to be? What kind of person do you want to be? It all starts *today* with good habits and discipline.

I know it may seem very dark right now. The hole of depression can be deep and can take on many forms. Maybe you feel unmotivated. Maybe you are sad. Do something to move yourself out of where you are and toward a healthier direction. Talk to somebody. Write in your journal. Go to church. Make a list of steps. Maybe you can only change one thing today. That's okay. Do that and build on it for tomorrow.

Take a minute right now to reflect on where you are, where you want to be, and how you can get there. For healthy people, *feelings* are the caboose of the train. The two cars in front of the train are *fact* and *faith*. Instead of being ruled by feelings, these people stick to the facts of their situation and rely on their faith to help them stand strong in the storm. Does this describe you? How might you benefit if you put fact and faith before your feelings? Ask God to help you see it all more clearly.

IN THE BEGINNING

In the beginning God created the heavens and the earth.

—Genesis 1:1 NIV

PRETTY BASIC STUFF, eh? But this is one of the most famous, most-loved passages in the Bible. Why is that? This is the very beginning as we know it. God has always been here and always will be here. But *we* haven't always been here. And we will go away in the blink of an eye compared to how long God has been in existence.

Think of it this way. Let's say you had a marker and you could draw a line on the wall all the way around the room in which you are sitting. Now pick a spot—any spot—on that line and make a dot. That dot represents your entire life, beginning, middle and end, in light of eternity.

This verse alludes to the fact that before God created, there was nothing. In fact, the next verse says, "Now the earth was formless and empty, darkness was over the surface of the deep" (Gen. 1:2). So the earth was just a planet of gas and matter with no order to it, with no forms like continents, and with no order such as days and nights, weeks, months, and years. There was no vegetation like trees or grass, and no moon and stars. There were no birds, no fish. There were no bugs, no wild animals. Nothing. Hard to imagine, isn't it? But just by speaking the words, God took this mass of nothing-ness and created order out of it.

If God can make order out of the chaos of an unformed planet earth, imagine what he can do with the chaos of our lives! All God had to do to bring birds and mountains and streams of water into being was *speak the words*. If we trust him and listen for his voice, he can begin making sense out of our chaos.

Won't you take a minute and ask God to bring order to your life? Listen to him and what he has for you. Rely on his power and his love to begin making sense out of your life.

ALL OF ME

God created human beings; he created them godlike, reflecting God's nature. He created them male and female.

—Genesis 1:27

BACK IN THE Garden of Eden, God created a lot of things. He created trees. And grass. And fish. And animals and plants. With each day, his creation became more and more complex. Then on the sixth day, God created man. Not just man, but man and woman. He created them in his image—*both* of them. Not just the man. Both genders reflect different aspects of God's nature. He created man to be masculine, to love an adventure and pursuit of a woman. He created woman to be nurturing, a warrior, and to hold an irreplaceable role. God did not create man with the woman as the default gender. Both genders were created in God's image. He created women on purpose, not as an afterthought.

We are surrounded by all types of messages to the contrary these days. Everywhere we look, we are bombarded with sexual messages, innuendo and sometimes just flat-out pornography. There seems to be no getting away from it. The problem is that the world has once again taken something sacred and holy and twisted it into a whole new meaning.

We are a package deal. God did not create us as separate parts but as a unified whole. God never intended for us to separate our body from the rest of us. He created us as uniquely male and uniquely female.

That means that my female-ness courses through my veins and through my thoughts, influencing my decisions, my parenting, and even my relationship with God. When women give their bodies to others to whom they are not married, it distorts God's plan and allows sin to enter the picture. What does that look like? Unplanned pregnancy, sexually transmitted diseases, and sexual addiction are just a few examples that come to mind.

In addition, it separates us from God. As Christians we are called out to be a holy people set apart for God. He created all of us and therefore he demands all of us—our whole person. We cannot serve God and be used by him when we are having sex with someone to whom we are not married. Our whole person needs to be on the same page. That doesn't mean we are perfect; it means we are submitting all of ourselves to God without holding back any part.

What are you holding back today? God wants all of you. Ask him now to show you what you are holding back from him.

NOAH AND
THE ARK

This is the story of Noah: Noah was a good man, a man of integrity in his community. Noah walked with God. Noah had three sons: Shem, Ham, and Japheth. As far as God was concerned, the Earth had become a sewer; there was violence everywhere. God took one look and saw how bad it was, everyone corrupt and corrupting—life itself corrupt to the core. God said to Noah, "It's all over. It's the end of the human race. The violence is everywhere; I'm making a clean sweep."
—Genesis 6:9-13

I LOVE THIS story of the big boat with all the animals and the big, beautiful rainbow God provided. Of course in the children's context, it all happens at one time and all of the animals are smiling. That probably wasn't how it was in real life.

I've always pictured the story of Noah like this: God told Noah to build a big boat. He gave him dimensions like height, length, and all the details. Then God told him to bring two of each kind of animal, male and female, onto the boat with him, Mrs. Noah, his sons and their wives. This is what we already know. But *why* did God tell Noah to build a boat? Because it was going to rain.

Before the Flood, the ground was watered from the bottom up. Underground springs supplied the water needed for crops, livestock, and other water needs. *No one in Noah's day had ever seen rain.* They didn't know what it was! So when God told Noah it was going to rain, this was a brand-new thing God was going to do. But did Noah question it? No. He simply believed and obeyed.

I've always wondered what Noah's neighbors must have thought. I mean, really! Noah was about 500 years old, building a boat in his backyard *for the coming rain.* His neighbors must have thought he was insane. And he didn't build this boat overnight. The Bible says Noah was 600 years old when the rains started. So if my math is correct, Noah was working on this boat for 100 years. Ha!

Sometimes God plants something in our hearts and in our minds that he is going to do. He speaks to us and molds us and prepares us for that thing. As humans, we tend to trust our eyes, and it's hard for us to believe that God is going to do something new and different from what we have ever seen before. We look around for somewhere else where God is doing something similar to what he has promised us. But we don't find it anywhere else because what he's doing in my life looks different than what he's doing in yours.

What is God doing in your life? What new thing does he want to do? What is he asking you to believe and obey and not question? Take a minute and reflect on Noah's life and yours.

GOD MEANT IT
FOR GOOD

Joseph replied, "Don't be afraid. Do I act for God? Don't you see, you planned evil against me but God used those same plans for my good, as you see all around you right now—life for many people. Easy now, you have nothing to fear; I'll take care of you and your children." He reassured them, speaking with them heart-to-heart.

—Genesis 50:19-21

JOSEPH HAD BEEN seriously wronged by his brothers. First they threw him into a deep well to die. But then a band of slave traders came along, and they instead sold Joseph into slavery for a profit. They took his coat, a special gift from their father, and covered it with goat's blood and told their father he was dead.

Fast forward twenty-two years. There is no food anywhere in the land, so Joseph's brothers go to the only place there is food, which is Egypt. Joseph is now second-in-command of the entire country and has been put in charge of the food distribution. Joseph sees his brothers coming and makes things a little rough for them at first, but he finally reveals himself to them and extends forgiveness for what they did to him. The brother they tried to kill is now their savior.

It doesn't matter where you are right now. You are smack dab in the middle of God's plan for you. Doesn't feel like it? Join the club. When we relinquish control of our lives to God, we no longer get to make decisions based on how they might make us feel or whether or not we'll be comfortable. God doesn't care about that. His eyes are on the big picture, and only he knows how to shape us and mold us to make us more like him. For me, it's through really tough times that I am forced to seek him more and more.

Maybe your church is falling apart. Maybe you are struggling financially. Maybe your marriage is in trouble. God uses different experiences to bring us closer to him. While it may feel like Satan is creeping in and taking control, it is ultimately God who has the last word.

Can you see good that has come out of hard times? Can you see how God could use the situation you're in right now for your good? Take a minute and thank God for loving you enough to use whatever means necessary to draw you closer to him.

THE CALLING OF MOSES

Moses was shepherding the flock of Jethro…The angel of GOD appeared to him in flames of fire blazing out of the middle of a bush. He looked. The bush was blazing away but it didn't burn up. Moses said, "What's going on here? I can't believe this! Amazing! Why doesn't the bush burn up?"…God said, "Don't come any closer. Remove your sandals from your feet. You're standing on holy ground…It's time for you to go back: I'm sending you to Pharaoh to bring my people, the People of Israel, out of Egypt." Moses answered God, "But why me? What makes you think that I could ever go to Pharaoh and lead the children of Israel out of Egypt?"

—Exodus 3:1-11

THE STORY OF Moses may be familiar to you. He is the baby who was placed in the basket in the Nile in order to escape the mandatory murder of all male children under the age of two. Think about the story of Moses this way. He was adopted into a life of power and privilege. It was Pharaoh's daughter who found Moses' basket and adopted him into her family as her son. The law said Moses should die, but God had something greater in mind for him. Kind of ironic that he would grow up in Pharaoh's household, isn't it?

As Moses grew up, God had great plans for him. Pharaoh ran him out of Egypt and he came to a new place. He was again adopted into a foreign family, got married and had children.

This is when God called him through the burning bush. He was about eighty when this happened. Although Moses didn't understand why God was choosing him, it kind of makes sense. Moses had grown up in Pharaoh's palace. He was deeply embedded in that family. But he also had a heart for the Hebrew people to whom he belonged by birth. He was the perfect choice to do the job.

Oftentimes God calls us to do a specific job that only we can do. While it's sometimes hard for us to see, there is no one else exactly like you in all this earth. God created you uniquely qualified to fulfill his call in your life. No one else has your set of experiences and choices and situations.

What is God calling you to do? Why do you think he's calling you to do it and not someone else? Take a minute to honestly reflect what he might be calling *you* to do.

MILK AND HONEY

Joshua son of Nun and Caleb son of Jephunneh, members of the scouting party, ripped their clothes and addressed the assembled People of Israel: "The land we walked through and scouted out is a very good land—very good indeed. If GOD is pleased with us, he will lead us into that land…And he'll give it to us. Just don't rebel against GOD! And don't be afraid of those people. Why, we'll have them for lunch! They have no protection and GOD is on our side. Don't be afraid of them!"

—Numbers 14:6-9

I N THIS PASSAGE, Joshua is addressing the Israelites. They are about to give up going into the Promised Land based on the information spread about the Amalekites and Canaanites and how big and powerful they are. The spies went into the land for forty days on a recon mission. Joshua and Caleb were among them. Those two were all for it and knew that if it was God's plan, the people could defeat anyone they needed to in order to make that plan come to fruition. But the rest of the delegation was freaked out by the opposition. They spread stories around the camp that it was too much for them to handle and they would do better to just turn and run the other way. The Israelites were so dramatic about their chances that they said things like, "Oh why didn't you let us die in the desert? Why did you bring us all the way out here to torture us like this?"

Who knows the mind of God? The day I read this I was heading into a meeting for a big project. There were many obstacles in the way, both seen and unseen. Yet, God kept reminding me that if this was his plan, if this was what he wanted to do, then he would make a way. Have you ever found yourself in this situation? Do you look at your life and see only obstacles?

As a result of the Israelites' lack of faith, God backed them up and put them in the desert. He actually wanted to kill them, but Moses was able to convince God that would be bad PR when the Egyptians found out that God had taken the slaves out of Egypt only to slaughter them in the desert. So instead of killing them, God turned them around and headed them into the desert. He vowed none of those who had grumbled against him would ever see the Promised Land. They would die first. Then he sent them into the desert one year for every day the spies were in the land of Canaan. Forty years. The trip to the Promised Land took mere months. God allowed them to go up to the border of the Promised Land only to back them out and turn them around because they didn't believe.

There are several lessons we can learn from this. The first is that if God is in something, then he can take care of whatever challenges come our way. I don't need to fear and I don't need to be afraid. Is anything too big for God? No.

The second is that God can and will change his mind if our attitude is not right. He brought the people *up to the border of the land* before turning them around. He fully intended for them to enter the land. But they began to gossip and worry and speak out against God's appointed leaders and he turned them around. God can do the same with us. Just because he promises us something doesn't mean he can't change his mind.

So the moral of the story is that God is in control but we still have free will. We can let God be God or we can take things into our own hands and be left to deal with the consequences. These are important lessons for us to learn. Take a minute and reflect on these in your own life.

DIVINE INSPIRATION OR MAGIC?

But the magicians of Egypt did the same thing with their incantations. Still Pharaoh remained stubborn. He wouldn't listen to them as GOD had said. He turned on his heel and went home, never giving it a second thought. But all the Egyptians had to dig inland from the river for water because they couldn't drink the Nile water.

—Exodus 7:22 NIV

MOSES HAD BEEN called by God to speak with Pharaoh and convince him to free the slaves. God promised Moses that he would be heard, and God even armed him with some miracles so Pharaoh would believe that God was indeed the one who had sent him.

But much to Moses' surprise, Pharaoh's magicians were able to do the same miracles. Moses turned a staff into a snake; the magicians did the same thing. Moses turned water into blood; the magicians did the same thing. Moses sent a plague of frogs over the land; the magicians did the same thing.

Here's my challenge for you: Just because something looks godly and looks like it's producing fruit doesn't mean it is. I want to encourage you to practice discernment at your church and in every aspect of your life. Just because something *looks* like a miracle designed by God doesn't mean it is.

The world is very savvy at making things "look" a certain way. Even churches are guilty of using slick marketing materials that highlight how

21

God is moving even if he is not. Don't be drawn in. Read your Bible. Test the spirits. If something doesn't feel right, ask God to reveal the truth to you. He'll do it. Take a minute and think about the different areas of your life. Is God truly present in all of them? Or does your life "look" good with no substance?

THE PARTING OF
THE RED SEA

GOD went ahead of them in a Pillar of Cloud during the day to guide
them on the way, and at night in a Pillar of Fire to give them light…
The Israelites walked through the sea on dry ground with the waters
a wall to the right and to the left. The Egyptians came after them in
full pursuit…Moses stretched his hand out over the sea: As the day
broke and the Egyptians were running, the sea returned to its place
as before. GOD dumped the Egyptians in the middle of the sea. The
waters returned, drowning the chariots and riders of Pharaoh's army
that had chased after Israel into the sea. Not one of them survived.
—Exodus 13:20-14:31 NIV

WHAT AN AMAZING scene this must have been. The slaves are
finally freed from Egypt after a series of plagues. The land has
been decimated by frogs, gnats, flies, boils, hail, locusts, and darkness.
Finally, God has killed every firstborn child in the land—from Pharaoh
all the way down to the animals. Egypt is in ruins physically, emotionally,
and spiritually. The slaves are free to go. While the plagues did not affect
the Israelites directly, it must have been a pretty overwhelming experience
to watch God show up and make those things happen on their behalf.

They leave Egypt in the middle of the night, and God takes them
to the Red Sea. Pharaoh, angry and hurting from the death of his son,
sends his armies after them. The slaves are trapped between the sea and
going back to a life of slavery. I wonder what they're thinking. Then

God shows up *big*. He blows a wind that separates the sea and *dries out* the land. Did you catch that? It wasn't enough to part the water; God also made sure the land was dry when they walked through.

Are you stuck between two seemingly bad options? I challenge you to try out faith. God knows exactly where you are, and he will show up big for you just like he did for the slaves. Take a chance and trust him today. Reflect on this story in your journal.

NO OTHER GODS

No other gods, only me.

—Exodus 20:3

THE TEN COMMANDMENTS are the most widely known list of rules in the world. Everyone has either heard of them or knows what they are, especially in America. They used to hang in our schools and our classrooms as well as in our churches. They've come under a lot of fire recently, and now people are not so sure the Ten Commandments should be displayed in public.

The truth is that before these rules were carved into stone tablets, they were written on the hearts of Adam and Eve. But then they ate the fruit from the tree that opened their eyes to sin, which negated all that God had built them for. And thanks to them, we are born sinners. Every one of us. If you are human, you are a sinner.

Knowing we are sinners, God had to give us rules—or boundaries— to live by. The first commandment is first for a reason. God wants to be first in our lives. Number one. Numero uno. The alpha dog. The premier. God is a jealous God. He is intolerant of unfaithfulness or rivalry.

God wants to be first in our lives because he created us and knows what is best for us. His plan often doesn't make sense to our human minds. I wrestle with that fact pretty much every day of my life. But he loves me and truly desires to have a relationship with me.

God wants you to know him and desire him more than anything else in this world. Only God can meet every need you have. Every good and perfect thing is from him and him alone. Oftentimes, God uses humans to comfort us and love us and meet our needs. But humans are always going to let us down. Always. Our boyfriends, parents, and friends will let us down.

God loves you and wants the best for you. He is perfect in every way. Won't you trust him and allow him to meet your needs this day? Ask him right now.

NO IDOLS

No carved gods [idols] of any size, shape, or form of anything whatever, whether of things that fly or walk or swim. Don't bow down to them and don't serve them because I am GOD, your God, and I'm a most jealous God...

—Exodus 20:4

I DON'T KNOW about you, but I don't sit around on my front porch carving wooden idols with a pocket knife. I don't whittle and I don't know how to use powered wood-working tools. Besides, what would be the point of carving an idol? It can't hear me when I pray or do anything about my requests. It can't see me, and it sure didn't create me. *I* created *it*.

Maybe back in Bible days, this was a concern. When Moses stayed on the mountain for forty days, receiving the Ten Commandments, the people got restless. Aaron collected their jewelry, melted it down, and formed the gold into a calf. Then the people sang songs to it and bowed down to it. How ridiculous is that?

It's obvious this particular commandment does not apply to us in this way anymore. But let's look a little bit deeper. How do you spend your time each day? If you wrote down how much time you spent working, eating, or shopping, where does most of your time go?

How about your finances? What do you spend the majority of your money on? Is it cosmetics? Clothes? Cars? Do you like to take fancy trips? Do you own a big, fancy house with all new furniture?

None of these things are inherently good or bad. What becomes a problem is when any of the above-mentioned things become more important than God. Do you spend so much money on one of those other things that you have no money left to give to your church? Are you so busy with travel or activities that you have no time to attend church services or Bible studies?

What are your priorities? The thing I know about priorities is that no matter what we say they are, our time and money know the truth. What we spend our time doing and what we spend our money on is proof positive of our priorities.

Do you need to rethink what's most important in your life? Do you need a priority adjustment today? Ask God to help you see what is most important in your life and to let everything else go.

NO CURSING

No using the name of God, your God, in curses or silly banter; God won't put up with the irreverent use of his name.

—Exodus 20:7

THANKS TO THE internet, text messaging, and instant messaging, we have become a society of lazy speakers and writers. Reading and writing used to be paramount to getting a job. You were judged on your cover letter and your resume before you even got a phone call. It wasn't necessarily the *content* of those things that mattered, but the fact that they were spelled correctly and used good grammar and proper punctuation.

Remember reading Shakespeare in high school? His use of language seemed awkward and hard to read and understand. Not only that, but schools love performing his plays, so speaking those words made learning the script feel like learning a whole new language.

Back in the beginning of writing, scribes would sit in the chamber of the king with a sheet of papyrus and an ink well. They wrote down everything that was said. The one exception was when talking about God. In the original manuscripts of the Bible, God was referred to by a group of letters instead of a word. YHWH is short for Yahweh and refers to God in Hebrew. God's name was considered so holy—and referred to so much power—that the Old Testament writers did not dare to even write out the whole name.

By contrast, we hear God's name used everywhere not as a holy and powerful name, but as a curse word. The God of the universe, who created each and every one of us in his own image, has been reduced to a curse word. It just seems so foolish.

This commandment clearly states that this is *not* okay. It was not okay in ancient times, and it is not okay today, even if everyone seems to be doing it. God will not stand for this. We may not see consequences today or tomorrow, but there is a price. If we are choosing to live a holy and pure life, the words that come out of our mouth have to change. God can have no part in sin. God cannot bless sin. And according to this verse, using God's name as a curse word is sin.

What words come out of your mouth? Are they pure and uplifting, or do they curse God? Take a minute and reflect on yourself. Ask God to help you have pure speech.

HOLY DAY

Observe the Sabbath day, to keep it holy. Work six days and do everything you need to do. But the seventh day is a Sabbath to GOD, your God. Don't do any work—not you, nor your son, nor your daughter, nor your servant, nor your maid, nor your animals, not even the foreign guest visiting in your town. For in six days GOD made Heaven, Earth, and sea, and everything in them; he rested on the seventh day. Therefore GOD blessed the Sabbath day; he set it apart as a holy day.

—Exodus 20:8-11

THE SABBATH IS a foreign concept to us. The line between the work week and the weekend keeps getting fuzzier and fuzzier. Monday through Friday is no longer the standard with shift work, part-time jobs and places that are open 24/7 such as Target, Wal-Mart and grocery stores. For some, a regular job isn't enough to pay the bills, so they have no choice but to work when they can. We have become a consumer-driven society that seems to push us all to work more so we can make more so we can spend more. And the cycle goes on and on.

When I read the Bible, I sometimes feel like it is out of touch with reality. They didn't have Target and Wal-Mart. They didn't have computers and the internet. They didn't have so many options of new homes and cars and clothes and…you get the idea. I wonder if Jesus *really* understands what it is like to have all the choices we have.

I think the answer is yes, Jesus *does* understand. The Bible talks a lot about money and how the things that captivate our pocketbooks are the things that will captivate our hearts. He wants us to be fixed on him and eternal things for a reason. He knows it is good for us.

So, what's the solution if you have to work every day? God was very up front when he commanded us to keep the Sabbath as a holy day. Growing up for me, Sunday was our Sabbath. It was set aside as a family day. We went to church, ate together, rested together, and played together. Later in the day we visited with our extended family. While I didn't think of it as a holy day, the fact that we had a day set apart for visiting was amazing. I hope to establish that tradition in my family some day.

Where are you in keeping a Sabbath in your house? What would you like to do differently? Take a few minutes and ask God what he would have you do. Ask him to help you do it.

HONOR

Honor your father and mother so that you'll live a long time in the land that God, your God, is giving you.

—Exodus 20:12

NO DOUBT YOU have heard this commandment before, probably when you were much younger. But did you know this is the first and only commandment with a promise attached to it? Not only should we honor our parents, but if we do we will live a long time. How do we honor our parents, especially if our relationship with them has been strained by our choices? If you are still living at home, honoring them includes giving them the respect they deserve, being obedient to their desires and wishes, following their rules, comforting them in their old age, and maintaining them if they need support.

If you no longer live at home, the relationship changes. While your parents are no longer over you as your providers and protectors, you can still be respectful of their views. Share things with them. Ask for their advice and be open to it. It doesn't mean they tell you what to do anymore, but you can show that you respect them by being open to their point of view.

If you are like me, your pregnancy changed your family forever. I joke that even after two decades, our family still hasn't recovered from my pregnancy. It has forever marred our perfect family and the idyllic life we once thought we had. My parents never wanted to talk about it, while my sister and I just started talking about that part of our lives in the last few years. It's strange how some families work through a major event like that and move on and others just get stuck. Of course, life kept moving forward, but the lack of communication and forgiveness surrounding that event has been like putting a boulder in the trunk of your car. It has weighed down the relationships and—for me—broken trust with my parents. I had nowhere to go with my hurt, grief, and anger. Unfortunately, I wasn't mature enough to realize I could take it all to God.

Maybe you have a story similar or worse. Given that hurtful past, how do we honor our parents? Well, it's a choice. We choose to honor them regardless of how they have treated us in the past or how they treat us now. This won't be easy, and it's not something we can do on our own. God has immeasurable power and strength and will give you what you need if you will only ask him.

My relationship with my mom has been tenuous at best. However, the last few years I have made an honest attempt to love her and honor her and see her as God sees her. I don't always succeed. But I keep going back to God and asking him to fill me and give me what I need. He never runs out of resources to help me. Won't you ask him to help you today? Take a minute and write in your journal.

NO KILLING

No murder.

—Exodus 20:13

THIS SEEMS SIMPLE and to the point, doesn't it? In most minds, murdering someone is the worst thing a person could ever do. Taking the life of an animal is bad enough, but taking the life of another *person*? It seems unforgivable.

As women, we are naturally life-givers. That is our role on this planet. It is how God put us together. We get pregnant and produce offspring. We nurse our babies at our breast. Lots of moms choose to stay home with their children and teach them while they are young and care for them as they grow up. Moms instruct kids about flowers and trees and friends and school. Our life-giving ability is not limited to our reproductive organs. While we can physically bear children, it is only the first step in helping them grow. We are made to be life-giving in everything we do.

Not murdering someone seems so easy in the physical sense. We live our lives and keep to ourselves and don't keep any weapons within reach, right? While in a moment of intense frustration we may think about killing the guy that cuts us off on the highway, we don't do it. The moment passes, a song we like comes on the radio and we're over it.

But not murdering someone with our words? That's a whole different challenge, especially for us as women. We're talkers. Unfortunately, we don't always use our words wisely. The Bible talks about the tongue as a two-edged sword that can spew life or death just by what we say. If we are life-givers in the way we are put together, how can we murder our friends or our enemies or family members by what we say?

Gossip. Slander. Lies. Do any of these sound familiar? We're all guilty. We disguise it as frustration or the need to "share" with a friend. My mom used to tell me that if I didn't have anything nice to say, I shouldn't say anything at all. That seemed a lot easier when my mom was looking over my shoulder reminding me of the difference between nice and not-nice talk.

Yes, this life is frustrating. It's hard and painful. We need to encourage and support and love one another through the hard times. But we need God more. He is where we need to go with our ugly words and thoughts. He can take them, forgive us for them, and help change the attitude of our hearts. Then maybe our words won't be quite as painful.

Take a minute and reflect on where you are and where you need work. Ask God to help you.

NO CHEATING

No adultery.

—Exodus 20:14

THIS IS THE seventh of the Ten Commandments and concerns our duty to ourselves and to each other. Adultery is having sex with someone to whom we are not married. It's cheating in marriage and premarital sex if we're single. It's having an affair, which makes it sound fun and exciting. And it is. Sex is fun and exciting. Sin is fun and exciting for a season—until the consequences start happening and it all falls apart.

Satan is so deceptive. Sin never looks like sin at the outset. It's always disguised as something else. Like a friendship. Or a kindred spirit. A soul mate. Someone who listens to me and understands me. It doesn't matter to us that this other person is married because *this isn't an affair*. It's a friendship. A work relationship. But the truth about relationships—any relationship—is that it's either growing or dying. Relationships are living beings and they don't stay stagnant. That is not the nature of relationships. So again, every relationship you have with another person is either growing or dying.

Many affairs don't start out as sexual. In fact, many affairs don't start out as affairs at all. They start out as relationships with other people: work people, church people, school people. Two people find in each other a friend, someone who understands what they're going through, a playmate. It usually starts out harmless. But since relationships are either growing or dying, the more you pour into a relationship, the more it's going to grow.

Physical affairs aren't the only thing we are in danger of. This commandment concerns the broader spectrum of chastity or living a pure, holy life. Sounds boring, doesn't it? God created us for his pleasure and his purpose. We cannot be used by God if we are not pure and holy and different from the world. We should be as much afraid of that which defiles the body as of that which destroys it. God can only use clean vessels. If we are not clean, he cannot and will not use us. We tie his hands from blessing us when we make decisions that are contrary to his teaching.

Do I mean clean like taking a shower? No. The Bible instructs us to be holy because God is holy. Holiness means to be set apart or different. Think about yourself for a minute. Is your life holy? Is it different from those around you? Do other people look at your life and see a difference from their own?

Take a minute and reflect on this. Adultery means much more than having sex outside of marriage. Ask God to help you understand how this applies to your life today.

NO TAKING WHAT DOES NOT BELONG TO YOU

No stealing.

—Exodus 20:15

THE THING I love most about the Bible is that it is as relevant today as it was 2,000 years ago. That's pretty amazing when you consider the technological advances that have occurred since then. Jesus didn't have a computer or a cell phone, yet it seems like he is referencing these things sometimes. Do you think that is possible?

"Do not steal" is a basic principle we all learn at a young age. We are taught to share our toys and not take a toy away from somebody who is playing with it. We're taught to keep our hands to ourselves and to not touch things that don't belong to us. And in this age of identity theft and computer fraud, here we are with a commandment from the literal dark ages that still holds true today.

What do you think? Do you think the Bible is relevant for us today? If so, how is this commandment relevant to your life? Maybe you are not a thief in the way that you break into someone's house and steal their television. But maybe you lie on your resume. Maybe you buy things on credit with no plan to pay them off. Maybe you get food stamps or some other type of help but you don't *really* need it. It just makes getting by a little bit easier.

This commandment is the law of love—loving others as we love ourselves and treating others as we ourselves want to be treated. It takes a lot of trust to live next door to someone. That trust is unspoken but known among neighbors. We have a certain responsibility to be an extra set of eyes and ears that pays attention to anything unusual that may going on in the neighborhood. We can only hope our neighbors are doing the same for us.

Ask yourself, is the Bible relevant to my life today? If so, consider what you are doing in your life that may be considered stealing in the light of this commandment. Ask God to make it clear to you how he wants you to fix it. Then ask him to help you make it right.

LOVE YOUR
NEIGHBOR

No lies about your neighbor.

—Exodus 20:16

H AVE YOU EVER had one of those neighbors you wish lived somewhere else? We've all probably experienced this at one time or another. My neighbors in college were too rowdy, even though I lived in the "quiet" dorm. My neighbors in the sorority house were too crazy. My current neighbors own two vicious dogs that I wish would get hit by a car. Nice, eh? Neighbors can surely bring out the good and bad in all of us.

So who are our neighbors? My first reaction is to name the people that live in the houses around mine. But that's not what Jesus said. A lawyer once asked Jesus that very question, "And who is my neighbor?" Jesus answered with a story. A man was beaten and robbed and left for dead by the side of the road. Two people passed by, including a priest, and did nothing to help the man. Finally, a third man came by who was of a different race. He helped the man, cleaned his wounds, and took him to a safe place to recover. Jesus said that this third man was a neighbor. So for us, our neighbor can be anyone with whom we come into contact at Wal-Mart, the grocery story, the mall, anywhere. The Bible says we should always be aware of those around us.

That covers the neighbor part of the verse. How about the lying part? Another Bible translation I like to use is the New International

Version. That version says, "You shall not give false testimony against your neighbor." That seems to cover a lot more than lying. We are to represent each other well. Living in a neighborhood requires a certain degree of trust. We trust that our neighbors will not break into our homes and steal our stuff the moment they see us drive away. We trust that in an emergency situation, our neighbors will help us if at all possible. We are to tell the truth about ourselves to our neighbors, as well as tell the neighbors the truth about the others. I'm not talking about gossiping here; I'm talking about portraying the other neighbors as they really are, not portraying them so we look good or better than we actually are. We are not to talk trash about our neighbors behind their backs. And since we have learned that our neighbor is anyone, this is how we are to behave in all situations.

Take a minute to reflect on how you treat people. Do you see yourself in any of the above descriptions either good or bad? Ask God to show you how you can be a better neighbor.

LUST

No lusting after your neighbor's house—or wife or servant or maid or ox or donkey. Don't set your heart on anything that is your neighbor's.
—Exodus 20:17

L UST. LUSTFUL. LUSTY. Such popular words right now. Isn't this what *Desperate Housewives* is all about? How about *The Bachelor?* I've never watched these shows, so I could be wrong, but this is the impression I get from the commercials. Lust is everywhere in our culture. It sells cars, drinks, clothes—you name it. Have you seen any music videos recently? We are an image-driven society, and visual imagery is the chief offender.

Lust is most closely tied with sex in its definition and origin. Other ways Webster defines "lust" is *an intense or obsessive desire; an overmastering desire.* Wow. That sounds powerful. Have you ever been under the spell of lust? It doesn't have to be sexual. I sometimes want to move to a different house so badly that it consumes me—my thoughts, my time, my efforts, my energies, and even my emotions. *That* is what lust is. Lust is desire run amuck.

Our neighbor is anyone with whom we have contact, anyone who lives in our neighborhood or someone we see at Target or the grocery store. The command is to not lust over *anything* our neighbor has. So it's not about wanting to sleep with our neighbor's husband, but it is about not wanting what they have. I think the phrase "keeping up with the

Joneses" applies here. This phrase refers to wanting what our neighbor has. We see they come home with a new this or that, and not only do we want it but the desire to have it consumes us. Interestingly enough, Webster defines "consume" as *destroy*. Hmmm.

God wants us to be consumed with him. The first commandment is "No other gods before me." God wants to be the one and only thing we desire. If we are so busy lusting after a newer car, a nicer home, cooler, hipper clothes, or a cuter boyfriend, then we are not going to have the energy we need to pursue God and a relationship with him.

Take a minute to reflect on your own life. Where are you on the lust scale? Do you desire God more than you desire anything else? What is coming between you and God? Ask him to help you overcome this obstacle to your relationship.

IS SEEING BELIEVING? OR "DON'T JUDGE A BOOK BY ITS COVER"

> "This bread was warm from the oven when we packed it and left to come and see you. Now look at it—crusts and crumbs. And our cracked and mended wineskins, good as new when we filled them. And our clothes and sandals, in tatters from the long, hard traveling." The men of Israel looked them over and accepted the evidence. But they didn't ask GOD about it.
>
> —Joshua 9:12-14

JOSHUA AND THE Israelites were successful warriors. They didn't sit around twirling their thumbs; they engaged in combat over and over. Time and time again, God gave them success. Each time before engaging in battle, Joshua would seek God, his plan, and his will. If God told Joshua not to do something, Joshua didn't do it. Remember that God's ways are not our ways. Joshua was the leader whom God instructed to march around the city of Jericho for six days before shouting on the seventh day. On that last day, the walls of the city literally crumbled to the ground. This was a man who knew God.

Maybe Joshua thought the Gibeonites were so clearly from a faraway land that he didn't need to ask God. Maybe he thought God had made it so plain and obvious that he would be wasting God's time praying and making sure. But the truth of the situation is this: the Gibeonites were their neighbors. They were afraid of Joshua and the Israelites and the God they worshipped—for a good reason. God had clearly been on the

Israelites' side and had helped them win amazing battles. So, instead of facing death at the hand of God's chosen people, the Gibeonites chose to submit themselves to Joshua and make a treaty with them. The only problem is that Joshua didn't ask God about it first.

So, what's the big deal? Joshua trusted what he could see with his eyes. As Christians, we need to be careful about this. Seeing isn't always believing. When Moses began performing miracles for Pharaoh, the ruler's magicians performed the same miracles. The only difference was that they drew their power from Satan, and Moses' power came from God.

What's the lesson here for us as believers? We can't trust ourselves or the world we live in. The wonder of technology makes anything appear possible. But our power and our hope are rooted in Jesus. We need to be aware of the difference between the power of God and the power of evil.

Do you trust your eyes? Are you willing to trust a God you have never seen in physical form and whose ways are different than ours? Take a minute and ask God to guide you. Ask God to reveal himself to you in a very personal way and then wait expectantly.

BITTER, PARTY OF ONE

> But she said, "Don't call me Naomi; call me Bitter. The Strong One
> has dealt me a bitter blow. I left here full of life, and GOD has brought
> me back with nothing but the clothes on my back. Why would you call
> me Naomi? God certainly doesn't. The Strong One ruined me."
> —Ruth 1:20-21

IS THIS HOW you are feeling today? Naomi had set out about fifteen years earlier with her husband, two sons, and two daughters-in-law. I'm sure she was also holding out hope for grandchildren, since that's what women did in those days—had babies. They had gone to a new land due to a famine in Israel, where they were living.

It wasn't long after moving that Naomi's husband died. Then she enjoyed ten years with her two sons and their wives. But at the end of ten years, both of her sons died and she was left alone in a strange land with two women related to her only by marriage. Of course she wanted to move back to her home, where she had roots and family and friends.

What strikes me about this story is two things. First, Naomi is bitter, bitter, bitter. She wants to change her name, and she blames God for taking away her family and dealing her what she calls a bitter blow. It appears there is nothing left of her faith in God, which makes me wonder how deep her faith was to begin with.

The second thing that strikes me about this story is her daughter-in-law Ruth. Ruth is also a widow; her husband is gone, too. Naomi begs Ruth to return home to her family, but she refuses. Ruth is faithful to her mother-in-law even though the woman is bitter and negative. Because of her actions, Ruth is grafted into the lineage of Jesus Christ. While we are all able to be "adopted" as children of God, Ruth actually has a place in the family tree because of her faithfulness to Naomi.

Which are you today? Are you bitter like Naomi, or are you more like Ruth? Are you able to accept what God has given you and remain faithful to him? Take a minute and ask God to reveal your heart.

BOAZ AS A PICTURE OF GOD

Then Boaz spoke to Ruth: "Listen, my daughter. From now on don't go to any other field to glean—stay right here in this one. And stay close to my young women. Watch where they are harvesting and follow them. And don't worry about a thing; I've given orders to my servants not to harass you. When you get thirsty, feel free to go and drink from the water buckets that the servants have filled."

—Ruth 2:8-9

WHAT A WONDERFUL story of provision! Ruth moved to a land where she knew no one, had no husband and no job. Her mother-in-law, Naomi, was a bitter old widow. Ruth took the responsibility of feeding herself and Naomi. She went out in a field to help harvest, without having a job. She totally trusted God to provide for her family. Even though she didn't know where she was going, God knew.

He led her to the field owned by Naomi's relative, Boaz. He gave Ruth permission to gather food there, but then he went a step further by offering her food and drink, and safety from the other workers. He didn't have to do that; in fact, many bosses in that day were harsh and would beat their slaves and take advantage of the women. But not Boaz. He was different.

He told Ruth that he had heard all about her and how she had refused to leave her mother-in-law. He had heard that Ruth had given up her own hopes and dreams to move to a strange land and learn a new way of life. He was very impressed with her character and told her so.

As it turned out, Boaz was a distant relative and could redeem the family name. He and Ruth married so that she would not be disgraced by being a widow and not having any children. The first child from Boaz would carry on the family name of Ruth's dead husband, Elimelech.

So, although Ruth made the hard decision to stay with her mother-in-law after the death of her husband, God blessed her in the end. The right decisions are not necessarily the easiest. Even though we can't see what is around the bend, our job is to trust God here and now without knowing what will happen next. God will honor our obedience to him. Just because we are choosing to follow God doesn't mean it will always make sense. In fact, it may never make sense! But God knows us better than we know ourselves, so we have to trust that he has our best interests at heart

Take a minute and reflect in your journal about all God is telling you right now.

OBEDIENCE

Here's what you are to do: Go to war against Amalek…This is to be total destruction—men and women, children and infants, cattle and sheep, camels and donkeys—the works…[Saul] captured Agag, king of Amalek, alive. Everyone else was killed…Saul and the army made an exception for Agag, and for the choice sheep and cattle…But all the rest, which nobody wanted anyway, they destroyed as decreed…

—1 Samuel 15:2-9

KING SAUL WAS a mighty warrior, a man anointed by God to be king and ruler. But all of that power went straight to his head. As soon as he became successful as a warrior, he stopped doing things God's way. Saul thought his ways were better and more effective.

In the scene recounted above, God had given Saul strict instructions through his prophet Samuel. There was no question that everything was to be destroyed upon capturing this city. But once the battle began and Saul was in charge, he took it upon himself to decide who lived and who died. At the end of the battle, God told Samuel he was sorry he had ever made Saul king. By the time Samuel got to Saul, Saul had slaughtered the animals as an offering to God. God could not receive this offering because Saul had sinned by keeping the animals in the first place.

You're probably wondering what the point of this is. It's funny how a situation that occurred thousands of years ago can have relevance to our daily lives. God gave Saul a job to do; he clearly laid out the details.

I believe God still speaks to us this clearly if we take the time to listen. Saul heard God, but he made up his own mind about which parts of the plan he was going to follow. As a result of these decisions, God took Saul's kingship away and plunged him into a deep depression.

Is God really God of your life? When he gives you a job, do you do it? Do you question it, or do you change it to fit into your life? God calls us to be obedient above everything else. He doesn't care about sacrifice or any other aspect of our lives the way he cares about obedience. Take a minute to reflect on this today. Ask God to give you the strength and courage to be obedient to him.

LOOKS AREN'T
EVERYTHING

> But GOD told Samuel, "Looks aren't everything. Don't be impressed
> with his looks and stature. I've already eliminated him. GOD judges
> persons differently than humans do. Men and women look at the face;
> GOD looks into the heart."
>
> —1 Samuel 16:7

DO YOU REMEMBER your mother telling you that looks aren't
everything? I do. Even at a young age, I didn't get it. Why wouldn't
she want me to be pretty? Why wouldn't she want herself to be pretty?
I danced with a dance company, and the emphasis was on costume and
make-up and hair. Wow! How completely damaging to a child! Of course
it mattered if we knew the dance steps and if we were dancing in unison,
but there seemed to be so much pressure put on looking grown up.

Isn't that our culture today? We live in an image-driven society. If it
looks good, it must be good. Did you know that even churches are judged
by how they package their messages? By how they present themselves to
the community? Aren't we as women judged by the style of our clothes
and hair? Look who we're competing with, though—women who have
professionals to style their hair and their clothes and their accessories;
women who are photographed and then edited in Photoshop to make
them look better, prettier, or sexier. Is that reality? You be the judge.

In this passage of the Bible, God has taken away the kingship from
Saul and is looking for a new king. He sends Samuel to the family of

Jesse in Bethlehem. Now, Jesse has eight sons. God tells Samuel to have Jesse introduce his sons to him one at a time. God assures Samuel that he will let him know which son is to be king. Samuel is overcome by the young men's looks and stature. All of Jesse's sons were handsome. Yet the first seven he introduced were not God's chosen.

Jesse failed to mention that not all of his sons were in attendance at this affair. The runt, David, was out tending sheep. His own father did not think enough of him to invite him to the event. So they called for David and sure enough, he was chosen by God.

What's the moral? Looks aren't everything, which is where we started. I'm just like you; I like to work out and fix my hair and put on make-up and wear fun clothes. *But it's not who I am.* Looking good and taking care of my body does not define me. To me, it is merely being a good steward of what God has given me.

Take a minute to reflect on these thoughts. Where are you today? Is your self-worth based on how you look? Or do you believe that God sees through all of that and judges you based on your motives and attitudes?

DAVE AND
THE BULLY

Saul answered David, "You can't go and fight this Philistine. You're too young and inexperienced—and he's been at this fighting business since before you were born."

—1 Samuel 17:33

THE STORY OF David and Goliath is a story between good and evil. I think God included this story in the Bible as an illustration of his own strength and power, not to boast or brag, but to help us have a better picture of who God really is.

David's job was tending his family's sheep and running errands for his father. On this day, David was bringing food to his brothers who were stationed with Saul's army. He overheard the giant bully, Goliath, threatening Saul's army, and David got mad. He knew that God had promised the land to the Israelites, who were in Saul's army. He was also angry because no one would stand up to the bully. Instead, all the soldiers cowered in fear.

David decided to trust God and do something about the bully. He took it upon himself to fight him, and he even told the giant that he was going to kill him and then cut off his head. But before David faced the giant, King Saul told him all the reasons why he couldn't win. Isn't that always the enemy's job—discouraging us, thwarting our plans with fear, telling us we aren't good enough, smart enough, or faithful enough?

David gives us a good example of what believing in God is really all about. He not only takes God at his word, he also puts actions to that idea. He believed to the core of his being that God wanted Goliath dead. He took a big risk by putting his own life in jeopardy to see that happen.

What is God telling you he wants to do in your life? What kind of risk is involved for you? What keeps you from stepping out in faith to take that risk? Ask God to help you trust him at his word, no matter what the odds are.

GOD'S WEAPONS ARE NOT MAN'S WEAPONS

Then David took his shepherd's staff, selected five smooth stones from the brook, and put them in the pocket of his shepherd's pack, and with his sling in his hand approached Goliath.

—1 Samuel 17:40

IN THE STORY of David and Goliath, David is facing a giant with much more size and much more experience in fighting. The king for whom David is fighting first outfits him with armor and a shield and a sword. David is a shepherd and not used to fighting with those types of weapons. He ends up taking the armor off because it is so heavy and bulky he is afraid it will weigh him down. Isn't that kind of ironic? The armor would have given him a better chance of making it out of the battle alive, but he was more concerned about being able to maneuver.

Instead of the armor, David opts for his shepherd's staff, five rocks and a sling. It doesn't sound like much compared to a ten-foot-tall giant clad in 126 pounds of armor, does it?

Here's the amazing thing about David's faith: Even though the odds were against him, he was sure of God. He was so sure of God that he selected five smooth stones from the brook. Why five? I think it's because he was so sure of God that he was willing to take out not only Goliath but also his four brothers if necessary. Sound like monster faith? It is.

How big is your faith? Are you willing to step out and trust that God is going to do what he says he's going to do?

There's a scene in *Indiana Jones and the Last Crusade* that has always stuck with me. Indy has to literally step out in faith when he crosses over the canyon and enters the cave where the knight is guarding the Holy Grail. When he steps out, the floor appears beneath him. It's actually quite powerful. This is what faith is. Not seeing the road clearly, with all its twists and turns, but trusting God that he will be there and will light each step along the way.

How big is your faith? Take a minute and reflect on this now. Ask God to help you have more faith. He will if you will ask him.

DEPRESSION

The next day an ugly mood was sent by God to afflict Saul, who became quite beside himself, raving.

—1 Samuel 18:10

HOW WOULD YOU say your mood is today? Are you happy? Sad? Peaceful? Depressed? King Saul obviously suffered from some kind of mood disorder. The Bible says that the reason Saul had these ugly moods was because the spirit of God had left him.

If you remember, Saul was unfaithful to God, and God was grieved that he had made him king. So God sent Samuel to find a new king, which he found in David. As soon as David was anointed, the ugly moods began to set in on the king, even though he was still on the throne.

My question is this: Where does depression come from? Therapists and counselors say that it is a hormonal imbalance that is genetic, that it is like diabetes and needs medicine to be brought back into balance. I don't disagree with any of this. However, what if the person who is suffering from depression submitted herself to God and began walking closely with him? What if that person prayed and spent time in the Bible every day? After living that way for a while, what if that person went to the psychiatrist? Would the symptoms be changed? Would the symptoms be different, not as dramatic?

As a therapist, I do believe in mood disorders. But I also believe that we are connected, integrated beings. Because of this, our spiritual life has an impact on the rest of our being. The Bible says that sin leads to death and wastes our bones. It also says that the shadow of our sin will overtake us. I believe sin to be a very powerful, serious force in our lives.

If you are a Christian, sin is a barrier between you and God. God cannot and will not tolerate sin. He can't even look at it. We need to be clean before God, and the only way to do that is to submit ourselves to God, pray and ask for his mercy and forgiveness regularly.

If you are not a Christian, sin is still keeping you from God. Confess your sinfulness to him and ask him to bring you into right relationship with him.

Let me be clear. Am I saying that if you are suffering from depression that it is punishment for your sin? No way. God doesn't work like that. However, I *am* saying that there are consequences for our actions. I want you to consider the fact that all parts of us are connected and that depression *may* be the result of some sin in your life.

Take a minute and reflect on this. Ask God to make you whole again.

TOO MUCH TIME
ON MY HANDS

One late afternoon, David got up from taking his nap and was strolling
on the roof of the palace. From his vantage point on the roof he saw
a woman bathing. The woman was stunningly beautiful.

—2 Samuel 11:2-5

D AVID WAS KING of the land, ruler over all he could see. God
had made him king and entrusted him with many servants and
soldiers, not to mention wives and children. He had just sent his soldiers
out to war, but instead of going with them, which was the normal thing
for a commander to do, he stayed home. We don't know why he stayed
home, but he did.

This is where the story gets interesting. If David would have done
what he was supposed to be doing, the next few chapters would have
never happened. Instead, he made his own way and his life got kind
of complicated. He slept with the woman whom he saw bathing, and
she became pregnant. In this story, David was actually in love with her.
Instead of trying to discredit her and claim he was not the father of her
unborn child, he immediately claimed the child as his own and had her
husband killed.

Have you ever heard the saying "Idle hands are the devil's workshop"?
Here is the proof. Maybe you've seen this in your life. Perhaps not to
this degree, but you are bored and have time on your hands. You think
your life is lacking and needs some excitement. So you turn on *Desperate*

Housewives. Or you go to the mall and spend money you don't have. Maybe you spend time with someone you know you shouldn't be spending time with.

It doesn't matter what the specifics are, the end is always the same. We need to protect our heart, soul, mind, and body from an enemy that wants to destroy us by pulling us off track, distracting us, or engaging us in some sin. As Christians, we need to set our minds on the things of God and ignore everything else.

So what are you dealing with right now? Do you have too much time on your hands? Is your life unstructured? Would a new job, a hobby, or a Bible study help add structure and discipline to your life? Take a minute to pray about these things. Ask God to show you his path and lend you his help.

SEX IS GOOD

Dear lover and friend, you're a secret garden, a private and pure fountain. Body and soul, you are paradise...

—Song of Songs 4:12

S ONG OF SOLOMON is the most sexy, exciting book in the whole Bible. Have you ever read it? The way the man and woman talk to each other, describe each other, and talk to their friends about each other is nothing less than R-rated. Or is it?

Sex was God's idea in the first place. It's not wrong to desire that connection with another. God created sex for our enjoyment and pleasure. It is the ultimate expression of our love for and commitment to another human being.

The problem is how we humans have messed it up. Sex was created to be enjoyed between one man and one woman for a lifetime. Don't believe me? Let's check it out. When a man and a woman wait until marriage to be together, what do they avoid? Sexually transmitted diseases, unintended pregnancies, jealousy from other lovers, baggage in the marriage. Hmmm...do you think maybe God had it right and *we* are the ones who have it wrong?

In this verse, the man is speaking to the woman. He is admiring her beauty, her sexuality, her *discretion*. "Secret garden" refers to her sexuality and her purity. Just because she is drawn to the man sexually doesn't mean she jumps into bed with him. She longs for him and desires him, but those feelings don't control her actions.

If you have messed up sexually, it's not too late for you. God blesses purity. Will it guarantee you a perfect life? No. But it will take many of the stresses out of it. Take a minute to reflect on where you are. Ask God to help you live a life of purity in all areas, including sexually.

JUST WHAT I NEED

Give us today our daily bread.

—Matthew 6:11 NIV

THIS THANKSGIVING MORNING as I was praying and trying in my own strength to make sense of my life, this passage occurred to me. Strange, since I don't usually pray the Lord's prayer. In fact, my prayers often sound more like senseless rambling. I find it hard to believe that God, the creator of the universe, never tires of my endless complaining, moaning, and questioning. How quickly I can tire of someone else's endless rambling. How short-tempered do I get when no one asks how I'm doing or what's going on with me? But not God. He doesn't expect that. He knows we're human and selfish by nature. After all, he created us, didn't he?

Anyway, back to my rambling. I was asking for something specific from God, a new way of dealing with a continual challenge. I honestly try not to ask for a specific thing very often because I'm smart enough to know how much I don't know. I've also seen in my life how I've asked for something, gotten it, but it has been far from the blessing I was hoping for. That's when this verse hit me. This is what God was saying as he was teaching his disciples. In my life I don't want riches or material things. The real truth is I don't know what I need. There's so much I don't understand, but I know the answer is God.

On this day, are you content in the knowledge that God knows what you need? Are you okay not knowing what you want or need? Do you trust him enough to care for you, his precious creation?

Have a blessed day.

TEMPTATION

Now Jesus, full of the Holy Spirit, left the Jordan and was led by the Spirit into the wild. For forty wilderness days and nights he was tested by the Devil. He ate nothing during those days, and when the time was up he was hungry. The Devil, playing on his hunger, gave the first test: "Since you're God's Son, command this stone to turn into a loaf of bread." Jesus answered by quoting Deuteronomy: "It takes more than bread to really live."

—Luke 4:1-4

ARE YOU EVER tempted to do something you know is wrong? Are you ever pulled to do something that may be wrong, depending on the circumstance? How about doing something that would feel really good but may reflect poorly on you?

I think we've all been in these situations. We each have been given free will by God. That means at any given moment we can choose to do anything we want to do. In or out of God's will. God does not intervene. He doesn't *want* to intervene. That's what happened in the Garden of Eden with Adam and Eve. They ate of the tree of knowledge of good and evil which clearly proves that from the beginning, we were created with free will. Now I personally hate having free will because I know what I am capable of doing. No matter how much I go to church or read my Bible or try to do the right thing, I have the ability to mess up my life in a heartbeat.

So, what's the solution for that? I point you to the Bible. In Luke 4, Satan takes Jesus out into the desert and tempts him. That's right, Jesus faced temptation. Satan tempts him with food. Crazy, right? We all have to eat. And I'm sure that after forty days of not eating, Jesus was hungry. So why does he respond the way he does? Because God is bigger than everything, including hunger. God can provide for our needs in many ways, *none* of which involve bowing to Satan and his demands. Jesus refused to come under Satan's authority even in the basic need of eating.

In this time of instant gratification, there are many options to getting our needs met. With technology we are able to make things happen quickly and easily. This is not God's way. He has a plan for your life and a timeline for your life. He doesn't need your help. He commands the universe and can make things happen without your intervention.

Take a minute and think about whether this describes you or not. Do you wait on God in prayer? Do you look expectantly for his answers to your needs and problems? Or do you ignore him and try to make things work out the way you want them to? Pick some issue in your life today and commit to waiting on God for the solution. You will be amazed at his timing and attention to detail.

THE CATCH

Simon said, "Master, we've been fishing hard all night and haven't caught even a minnow. But if you say so, I'll let out the nets." It was no sooner said than done—a huge haul of fish, straining the nets past capacity.

—Luke 5:5-6

H AVE YOU EVER tried your hardest to accomplish something with no success? Have you ever worked your tail off for a promotion or worked on a project so hard only to be denied the praise you were seeking? That's what Simon was experiencing here. He had been fishing all night long with no luck. He was a fisherman by trade, so more than likely no fish meant no pay.

Now he's back from a luckless night of fishing. He's tired and has nothing to show for his efforts. Here comes his friend Jesus and asks to sit in Simon's boat while he teaches the people. At the end of Jesus' message, he instructs Simon to go into deeper water and let down the nets for a catch.

That's when Simon responds with the above verse. If I had to guess, I would think that the last part, "But if you say so…" was said with a bit of sarcasm. Simon had been letting down his nets all night with no luck. But now because Jesus says so, he's going to get a different result?

Exactly. This was exactly according to God's timing. How many times in my life have I done the right thing at the wrong time? Let me put it another way. I have done the right thing on my own timeline. I have been too impatient to wait on God and instead took things into my own hands. Or the opposite has been true. I have heard what God said to me, but I waited to do it until it fit into my timeline. I thought, "Yeah, that's a good idea. But I will do it when it seems right to me."

God's ways are not our ways. His timing will not always make sense to us. But it makes sense to him, and isn't that what's important? He can see the big picture. He can see the past, the present, and the future. Shouldn't we trust him to know what's right for us at the right time?

Take a minute and reflect on this. Are you committed to doing things God's way the first time? Ask God to help you trust him more.

INVISIBLE WAR

"This is war, and there is no neutral ground. If you're not on my side, you're the enemy; if you're not helping, you're making things worse."

—Luke 11:23

G OD'S WORD SPEAKS to us very plainly about the life we are currently living. For many of you, life may be a series of ups and downs, joys and sorrows. But God has a bigger plan than that. This is a war, not so much like the wars America has fought in years past, but more of an unseen war.

At any given time there are angels and demons all around us, fighting for the possession of our soul. I'm not trying to scare you and no, I'm not crazy. I know this sounds like some scary movie. But it is the truth. Satan wants to own us, and the way he does that is by watching us and getting to know us so he can know our weaknesses. Once he knows our weaknesses, he knows how he can trip us up, how he can tempt us, and how he can make us stumble. By continually keeping us caught in a cycle of messing up and trying to do better, he renders us ineffective for the kingdom of God.

For us Christians, our challenge is to keep our eyes firmly fixed on Christ, no matter what. Instead of riding the waves of ups and downs, we need to chart a steady course, where we trust God *no matter what happens* to us, our business, or our family.

This is a war, and there are only two sides. Being a "good" person won't cut it. You are either a believer in Christ or you're not. Take a minute and reflect on where you are right now. Have you accepted Christ as your personal Lord and Savior? If not, do that right now. If you have, write down how you could be living a steadier life in the midst of your circumstances.

A GOD OF
CONTRADICTIONS

You're blessed when you've lost it all. God's kingdom is there for the finding. You're blessed when you're ravenously hungry. Then you're ready for the Messianic meal. You're blessed when the tears flow freely. Joy comes with the morning.

—Luke 6:20-21

I T IS HARD for us as human beings to even begin to comprehend God. When we first become Christians, we see him as a loving, merciful Lord who took away our sins on the cross. But it seems the longer I know him and walk with him, the less I truly comprehend him. The more I get to know his sinlessness and perfection, the more I recognize my own sinfulness and imperfection.

This is exactly the teaching of Jesus. We have to lose our life in order to save it. He had to die in order for us to live in eternal life. Everything has to die and rise again. Think about the tulips and the trees. They die in the winter and lay dormant until the right time, when they sprout to life again. We are blessed when we are suffering or hurting in any way. It doesn't make sense to us, but it does to God. He knows who we are on the inside, and he knows what we need in order to be perfected. This world is simply a preparation for the next. Not an afterlife-type of world, but heaven. Those of us who have accepted Christ will go to heaven and have jobs and assignments. We are being prepared for that now.

Take a minute and look at your life through God's eyes. What seems unfair to you right now? What seems hard or painful? What could possibly be gained by going through this right now? Ask God to help you trust him during this season of your life.

HEART AND MOUTH

You don't get wormy apples off a healthy tree, nor good apples off a diseased tree. The health of the apple tells the health of the tree. You must begin with your own life-giving lives. It's who you are, not what you say and do, that counts. Your true being brims over into true words and deeds.

—Luke 6:43-45

D ID YOU KNOW your heart and your mouth are connected? Obviously they are both vital parts of your body. You wouldn't be walking and talking without your heart pumping blood through your veins and organs. And talking, singing, eating, and drinking would be difficult without a mouth.

But beyond those obvious attributes, the heart and mouth are connected in another way. The Bible says that who we are is seen through our words and actions. To get that point across, God uses the illustration of a tree and its fruit. What counts to God is character, not behavior. We can't be good people by *doing* the right things. Sure, it's good to do the right thing. But that doesn't make me a good person. We aren't going to spend eternity in heaven because we do the right thing. God wants our hearts to be clean and pure before him, and the only way to do that is to invite Jesus to come in and clean house and be Lord of our lives.

Let's say you have a healthy tree that you water and prune and fertilize and feed good tree food. The tree is without disease or defect of any kind. What kind of fruit do you think will come from this kind of tree? Probably good, healthy, juicy fruit.

The same is true with your heart. If you invite Jesus into your heart to clean house and fill your heart and mind with good fertilizer like the Holy Spirit, the Bible, a good solid church, clean activities and living, the chances are good that what is going to come out of your mouth and your life will be good and true and pure naturally. You won't have to *try* and change your behavior; it will change on its own as your heart is being changed!

Take a minute to reflect in your journal about today's thoughts. What kind of fruit is coming from your life? How would you like for it to be different? Ask God to help you.

THE GOOD
NEIGHBOR

A Samaritan traveling the road came on him. When he saw the man's condition, his heart went out to him. He gave him first aid, disinfecting and bandaging his wounds. Then he lifted him onto his donkey, led him to an inn, and made him comfortable. In the morning he took out two silver coins and gave them to the innkeeper, saying, "Take good care of him. If it costs any more, put it on my bill—I'll pay you on my way back."

—Luke 10:33-35

YOU'VE PROBABLY HEARD the jingle for State Farm insurance "And like a good neighbor, State Farm is there." This is the story of that song. When you think of your neighbor, what immediately comes to mind? The first thing I think of is the families that live to the right and left of my own home. Then I think about the people across the street and down the street. But this story, and even the jingle, are about a different type of neighbor. This story is about a man who was beaten and left for dead and another man who wasn't his neighbor at all.

The man who was beaten was a Jewish man. He was on his way to Jericho when robbers came upon him and robbed him. Soon after this happened, a priest came down the road. Lucky for the man, eh? Or not. He refused to help him even though the man was bloody and probably unconscious. Maybe the priest thought he was dead. Maybe he was late for a meeting.

The second man was also a leader in the church. Lucky for the hurt man, eh? No again. This person also passed him by and looked the other way.

It wasn't until a Samaritan man came down the road that the first man got any kind of help. The Samaritan not only helped him, but took him to a safe place so he could recover and heal before going on his way.

The important part of this story is that the Samaritans and Jews hated each other passionately. Yet none of that mattered when one person saw another person hurting.

What's in this story for us? A lot! We discriminate in so many ways besides skin color. Age, ability, physical features. How do you discriminate? Take a minute to ask yourself. Then ask God to help you change and see people for what they really are...God's creation.

BEING VS. DOING

It's who you are and the way you live that count before God. Your worship must engage your spirit in the pursuit of truth. That's the kind of people the Father is out looking for: those who are simply and honestly themselves before him in their worship. God is sheer being itself—Spirit. Those who worship him must do it out of their very being, their spirits, their true selves, in adoration.

—John 4:23-24

HAVING GROWN UP in the church, I often associate worship with music. I think of having worship and praise time with a team, a choir, or an individual on a stage with a band, piano, or some kind of music. That is what the word worship means to me.

Now that I have grown up a little, I understand worship to mean something much bigger. Jesus wants us to have an attitude of worship all the time. He wants everything we do to be for him and about him. God doesn't see worship as an isolated event; rather, he sees worship as a way of life.

This passage is part of the story of the woman at the well. Jesus had been traveling and stopped for a drink in the middle of the day. He was surely hot and tired from walking such a long distance. In those days, prejudices ran deep. Jesus was Jewish while the woman was of Samaritan descent. So when Jesus asked the woman to give him a drink, she was shocked that he would even speak to her. Jesus began telling her about faith in God and how that would change her life.

Jesus emphasized *being* over *doing*. It's so easy to get caught up in the busyness of serving at church. It's great to teach Sunday school class or sing in the choir or greet people as they walk in the door. Churches always need help ushering or parking cars or working in the bookstore. These things can make Sunday mornings hectic, busy, and *stressful.* God didn't mean for church to be a stressful event. It's supposed to be enjoyable as we fellowship together, sing together, and learn more about the Bible together.

Do I think it's wrong to serve in a church? Of course not. God commands us to be part of a local body of believers, the church, and to use our gifts to serve the church. It's not about duty—doing something because we *have* to—but about a calling, doing something because we have a desire to serve in that way.

God told the Samaritan woman that being is more important than doing. I believe he is telling us the same thing today. Take a minute and inventory your busyness with church and with your everyday life. Ask God to help you see what you are doing out of duty versus what you are truly called to do.

THE TRUE VINE

I am the Vine, you are the branches. When you're joined with me
and I with you, the relation intimate and organic, the harvest is sure
to be abundant. Separated, you can't produce a thing.

—John 15:5

I WAS LOOKING at a large pear tree today. If you've seen these
mature trees, they have a very distinctive leaf shape that is pointed
on top and rounded through the body to the stem. They are just beautiful. There was something funny about this tree, though. Half of the
leaves—from top to bottom—were all the way out, green and fluttering
in the breeze. But the other half of the tree was just starting to bud. I
stared at it for a minute because it was perfectly split down the middle.
It made me wonder why it looked like that. Then I noticed the sun. One
half of the tree received more direct sunlight than the other half. It was
such an odd sight, but it made me think of my spiritual life.

Why is it that in some areas of my life I have full-grown leaves and
other areas of my life are just buds? I think the difference may be exposure
to direct sunlight. God created us with free will. We can choose to receive
him into our lives or not. Once we receive him into our lives, it is still
up to us to surrender everything—each area of our life—over to him.
This is a process and not something that necessarily happens overnight.
By surrendering an area of our life over to God, we are giving him the
authority to shine his light into that area and get rid of the garbage.

While the light of God's love reveals things in us that may need to be changed, it also allows that area of our lives to grow. Just like the light from the sun is for seeing and for growing, so is God's light.

Like the branches to the vine, we have to be connected to him. By inviting Jesus into our heart and life, we invite his sunlight to pierce us to reveal what needs to go and what needs to grow.

Have you invited God into your heart? Have you surrendered every part of yourself to God? Have you welcomed his life-changing light into the deepest parts of yourself? Take a few minutes and ask God to help you go deeper with him.

SLIPPERY SLOPE

You are dead to sin and alive to God. That's what Jesus did. That
means you must not give sin a vote in the way you conduct your lives.
Don't give it the time of day. Don't even run little errands that are
connected with that old way of life. Throw yourselves wholeheartedly
and full-time—remember, you've been raised from the dead!—into
God's way of doing things.

—Romans 6:11-14

THE BOOK OF Romans is a letter written by a man named Paul to
people in the church in Rome. His passion was for people to come
to know God in a very personal way. We live in a very "churchianity"
culture, where people go to church on Sundays and then live the way
they want for the rest of the week. Paul saw salvation and a relationship
with Jesus as something to be lived out every day of the week. Romans
talks a lot about what that looks like and how to do it.

One thing I really like about Paul's writing is that he is so real and
relevant, even today. He acknowledges that the devil is real and is all
around us. Satan is our very real and mighty enemy, and we always
need to be on guard. Paul repeats many times that if we call ourselves
Christians then we are dead to sin. Dead to sin? Does that mean that we
are unable to sin? No. By committing ourselves to God, our old nature
is replaced with the Holy Spirit who takes control of our lives. Being
dead to sin means that by becoming a Christian, sin loses its hold and

appeal over us. Of course as humans, we will always have the opportunity to sin. While our spirit may be dead to sin, our flesh is still very much alive and always looking to satisfy itself.

The tricky thing about sin is that it doesn't always look like sin to the casual observer. Satan is very deceptive that way. Is taking a drink of alcohol wrong in God's economy? Of course not. Is it wrong to have lunch with someone who isn't a Christian? No. But as Christians we are called to be wise as serpents. We are called to be holy and set apart from the rest of the world. While it may not be wrong to do some things, we need to recognize the bigger picture of where they could lead. Does having lunch with a non-Christian lead to a relationship when we are not to be yoked with a non-believer? Where does a drink lead for you? To more drinks? To out-of-control behavior? We have to be very careful of our actions and be aware of where they may lead.

Part of this verse says, "Don't even run little errands that are connected with that old way of life." Our old life was before we became Christians. No matter how long it has been since you came to Christ, it's important to be on guard. Sin can be disguised as something innocent. If we aren't careful, we can suddenly find ourselves thrown back to our old ways.

Where are you today? Ask God to help you recognize sin no matter what the packaging.

LIVING SACRIFICES

Take your everyday, ordinary life—your sleeping, eating, going-to-work, and walking-around life—and place it before God as an offering. Embracing what God does for you is the best thing you can do for him. Don't become so well-adjusted to your culture that you fit into it without even thinking. Instead, fix your attention on God. You'll be changed from the inside out. Readily recognize what he wants from you, and quickly respond to it. Unlike the culture around you, always dragging you down to its level of immaturity, God brings the best out of you, develops well-formed maturity in you.

—Romans 12:1-2

THE BIBLE SAYS we are to be living sacrifices. What exactly is that? It's not the slaughter-the-bull-on-the-altar sacrifice that we read about in the Old Testament. The above definition is pretty modern.

In the old days, they used to slaughter animals outside on a big stone altar. That worked fine because the animals died. The problem with being a *living* sacrifice is that we can choose to crawl off the altar. My little girl loves to sit on my lap and snuggle. She loves me to rock her and sing to her...for a while. Then she loses interest in me and gets distracted by her toys. It isn't long until the toys have caught her eye and she is crawling off my lap.

How much is that like us? We commit ourselves to God and his works and plans. We promise to stay in his will—whatever *that* means.

That is until something else catches our attention and we're off in another direction.

God tells us that *all* of our lives are to be a sacrifice: sleeping, eating, and working included. He wants us to come to the place where we realize this world is not our home. Sure, this is where we live and work and play and marry, but this is not our eternal home. We were created to live forever. Did you know that? Seventy or eighty years does not a forever make. Our lifetime is simply a dot on the continuum of eternity. We will spend more time in heaven or hell than we ever did on earth.

The Bible constantly encourages and challenges us to listen to God and be obedient immediately. God knows how quickly our lives pass and we are gone. Take a minute to reflect on these thoughts. Are you living as a sacrifice to God? Or are you living for yourself? Ask God to help you live more and more like him.

SEEING CLEARLY

We don't yet see things clearly. We're squinting in a fog, peering through a mist. But it won't be long before the weather clears and the sun shines bright! We'll see it all then, see it all as clearly as God sees us, knowing him directly just as he knows us!

—1 Corinthians 13:12

I RECENTLY BOUGHT a play kitchen at a yard sale for my little girl. I was excited to find such a bargain, regardless of how dirty the thing might be on the outside. I could get it clean! I scrubbed and wiped and scrubbed and wiped. With each pass of the cloth, it came cleaner and cleaner. Each crack and crevice and corner was just waiting for my rag and the scrubbing action of the scum-buster. The colors grew more brilliant as the cleaning continued.

The funny thing was that at first it didn't look all that dirty. It had obviously been well-used, but it wasn't disgusting by any means. I don't mind buying used things for my child; she's just going to beat them up anyway. But once I started scrubbing and cleaning, it became more and more clear how dirty this play kitchen really was. Although it was tough to see at first, it became obvious that it had been stored in the garage and had a thick layer of dirt and grime over the whole thing. But I couldn't see it until I started cleaning it.

Spiritual application? You betcha! I began thanking God for His patience with me. I began thanking Him for taking the time to make sure He got every crack and crevice and corner clean in me. God wants us healthy and whole, and only He can do that. It takes time and work and lots of effort. And we have to be willing. If we are, God can get in there and get us spotless.

This verse says, "We're squinting in a fog, peering through a mist." I couldn't see how dirty the kitchen was until I started to clean it. Left to my own devices, I am clean and pure and holy. It's only when I start looking in the mirror of the Bible that I begin to see how prideful and selfish and sinful I really am. The kitchen is clean now and my little girl loves it. God continues working on my heart, and I expect it to be a lifetime of work.

Take a minute to reflect on your own life. Are you truly clean inside and out? Or do you have a veneer of grime on you that is tough to see? Ask God to help you be truly clean before him.

A LIGHT TO MY PATH

By your words I can see where I'm going; they throw a beam of light on my dark path. I've committed myself and I'll never turn back from living by your righteous order. Everything's falling apart on me, GOD; put me together again with your Word.

—Psalm 119:105

RECENTLY WE HAD new garage door openers installed on our home. We upgraded from the old ones and they now require much less maintenance. They are also quieter and fancier. We even got an outdoor keypad so the next time I lock myself out of the house, I won't have to call anyone for help.

The best feature of the new doors is the motion sensor on the garage lights. Instead of fumbling for the light switch or having to open one of the doors to get light, all I have to do is step into the garage and the lights switch on. The trick is that the sensor has to see me; that is, I have to be in front of the sensor for the light to click on. That means I have to step into the darkness before the light comes on.

Is this not what walking with God is all about? Have you ever thought about that? Why is the Word only a lamp to my feet? God only needs us to see and do what he has put right in front of us. We don't need to know the big picture, and seldom do we. God just wants us to trust him with what he has given us. Sometimes that means stepping into the darkness before the lamp clicks on to light our way.

It seems like there are many days when I am drowning in darkness. I pray and ask God to reveal his work to me, and I don't see anything. But I can see the day I'm in—the step I'm on, if you will—and that is enough. We don't know what the future holds. We don't even know what tomorrow holds. But if we are believers in Christ, we know *who* holds all of our tomorrows; we just have to trust in him.

Do you believe God created you for a purpose? Do you believe all of your steps are ordered by him and that he is not leaving you alone, abandoned? Rather, he wants you to trust him even when things are unclear; *especially* when things are unclear.

Take some time to write in your journal and reflect on this. Do you believe it? Do you want to believe it but are having a hard time doing so? Ask God to help you trust him more and more. Ask him to reveal himself to you.

SEA STARS

I'm feeling terrible—I couldn't feel worse! Get me on my feet again.
You promised, remember?

—Psalm 119:25

RECENTLY OUR FAMILY took a vacation to Cannon Beach, Oregon. This beach is out on the Pacific coast about where the ocean meets a huge river. In the middle of this beach is a huge haystack formation of rock that stands several stories high. The base of the rock is submerged in water when the tide is high.

One morning I got up before anyone else and walked down to the beach to investigate. I was unfamiliar with the Pacific coast's rocky shoreline and was intrigued by this gigantic rock. It was cold and foggy as I made my way. My timing was perfect. The tide was out and heading back in.

As I neared, I noticed people milling about the bottom of Haystack Rock. They seemed to be looking at something. I followed the people and soon saw what all the excitement was about. The tide was out, but thousands of sea stars and anemones had been left behind. They were clinging to the rock, clinging to each other, some only attached by one leg. They were literally clinging to life on those rocks. They were orange, red, purple, big, little, fat, skinny. I had never seen so many starfish at once; in fact, I had never seen so many—period!

I asked one of the naturalists if they were dead. He said they were able to survive for a few hours at a time without water. He explained that as long as they were securely fastened to the rock, they would be fine. "What about those that have only one leg attached?" I asked. He said that as long as any part of their body, no matter how small, was attached to the rock, they could make it until the tide came back in.

I don't know if you know this, but sea stars can regenerate limbs. This means that if they lose one of their legs for some reason, they can grow another one and keep right on living. So as long as they are alive, they can regrow lost limbs.

Those sea stars clung to that rock or faced death. Every few hours, the water came back and brought them food and life. If they weren't connected to the rock, however, that was the end of them.

Is Jesus Christ your lifeline today? Have you let him into your heart and life and committed yourself fully to him? How different your life will be if you take this one leap of faith. Let him be your source of life today. Take a minute and ask him to refresh you.

CONTROL

Delight yourself in the LORD and he will give you the desires of your heart.

—Psalm 37:4 NIV

CONTROL IS AN illusion. Have you ever noticed that? No matter how hard we try, control is elusive. When we are hurting or anxious, we control what we can: we control our hair and makeup or the clothes we wear. We control the appearance of our home or our car. We control how other people see us by acting a certain way or saying certain things. For some of us, we control our environment by cleaning our house, picking up every stray item and cleaning every spot of dirt.

After my daughter was born, I controlled how other people saw me. My family didn't want to talk about my baby or "the pregnancy." We moved away from everyone I had ever known. I acted like it didn't matter. I joined the cheerleading squad at school. I wore the "right" clothes and said the "right" things. I was smart, so I knew the "right" people.

But on the inside, I was falling apart. I had no one to confide in, no one who knew about that part of my life who would talk to me and nurture me and love me. The family that did know about that part of my life wanted to act like it had never happened. So I acted that way too.

My relationship with Jesus was very new and I was still learning what it meant to walk with him and know him and love him. I was trying to live for him, but what did that mean? We went to church every week, but I didn't fit into the youth group. I was different now, but still inside a teenager's body. I clung to the above verse. I didn't know what it meant exactly, but I was learning.

Maybe you're still exploring a relationship with God. Maybe your relationship with him is new. Wherever you are, God hears you. He sees you and knows you. You are not alone. Do not despair. He created you and he loves you. All the good parts, the bad parts, the sad parts, he loves everything about you. There is nothing you can do that will make him not love you.

Take a minute and pour out your heart to Jesus. He loves you and wants a relationship with you above everything else. Won't you trust him with your heart today?

OUR ONLY HOPE

Blessed is the man who does not walk in the counsel of the wicked or stand in the way of sinners or sit in the seat of mockers. But his delight is in the law of the LORD, and on his law he meditates day and night...For the LORD watches over the way of the righteous, but the way of the wicked will perish.

—Psalm 1:1-2, 6 NIV

I T SOUNDS LIKE a recipe, doesn't it? That if I just do the things on this list, God will love me and accept me and let me go to heaven. The problem is that God is not a God of *doing*, but a God of *being*. He wants us to do the things in the verse not because we want to or have to or even because they are the right things to do. He wants to see these things in our lives as a result of time spent alone with him in quiet, reflective devotion. God wants our lives, not our behavior!

God desires to bless our lives. He created us and loves us like no human can. God has the ability to see into our hearts—into the depths of our souls—and see who we really are. He sees the truth of ourselves, something that most of us don't want to admit to knowing about. Some of us are so jaded that we don't even know what is lurking about in our own souls. But God doesn't have to wonder about that; he sees it. Yet he loves you and cares for you like no one else ever could. He died for you so that in spite of your hate and selfishness and loneliness and hurt you could still go to heaven and spend forever with him. All you have to do is believe in him. That doesn't sound too hard, does it? But it's very hard for so many people.

Even now as a healthy grown-up, there are very few people in my life whom I tell everything to. It's not that I'm pretending or acting, but there are things that I still don't like about myself, so why should I think anyone else would be able to accept them? It's not things like "I think that girl's dress is ugly"; it's more like "I *want* my friend's house because it's nicer." Ugly, nasty stuff is lurking in my heart and soul. How did it get there? I was born this way. I'm an ugly, nasty person. We all are. This is what happened to us when Eve and Adam ate the fruit from the forbidden tree in the Garden of Eden. This ugliness entered into the world and into our hearts. It's in all of us.

Our only hope is Jesus. Our only hope is to throw ourselves at the foot of his cross and ask him to heal us, to forgive us, and to love us in spite of ourselves. Do you know there is nowhere you can run to that is too far for God to reach you? Take time with him right now. Ask him to open your eyes to the sin in your heart and your life. Ask him to clean it up and help you start seeing him with cleaner, fresher eyes.

GOOD, BETTER, OR BEST?

Now you've got my feet on the life path, all radiant from the shining of your face. Ever since you took my hand, I'm on the right way.

—Psalm 16:11

HOW MANY OF you ask God to lead and guide you each and every day? Even after we have made the choice to walk with Jesus, it seems like every day we have many choices and endless decisions to make for ourselves and our families. Making the decision to become a Christian is supposed to make the rest of our life easy, right? Becoming a Christian takes the guess work out of whether or not we are going to break the law by speeding or robbing a store or drinking a lot of alcohol. So by taking those examples further, becoming a Christian should make other choices in our lives simpler too, right?

Not exactly. While it is true that asking Jesus to be our Lord and Savior sets us on a new path, it doesn't necessarily make every decision as plain as day. I was walking recently in our neighborhood. When I turned around and looked behind me at the sidewalk I had just walked on, I could see the whole block of the sidewalk and all the deviations from the main path for driveways and mailboxes. That's kind of what being a Christian is like. Since we still have free will, we can choose to stay on God's path or get off at any time. While being a Christian sometimes makes our decisions super easy, other times they are not so clear.

We have to keep in mind that our enemy, the devil, prowls around looking for our weaknesses. He sometimes even masquerades as an angel of light. What that means for us is that we need to stay close to God by spending time with him every day, asking his wisdom in every circumstance and praying for discernment. That way, when the devil is trying to trick us, we will have an open line of communication with God so he can speak to us and warn us.

Many times the decisions we are faced with are not between right and wrong. Those are the easy ones! Instead, they are between good and best or between good and God. What's the difference? Serving in your church or community is a good thing. But if God is not calling you to do that, then you would be stepping outside of his will to do it. Even though it may be a good thing to do, it may not be right for you.

We need to stay so close to God that we ask him about everything. While doing good is okay, doing without God's power will leave you weak and inefficient in that area of service. Wouldn't you rather go where God says you should go and succeed?

Ask God right now to start showing you the areas of your life where he is not calling you. Then ask him to show you the areas where he is calling you. Ask him for strength and courage to step out in faith in these areas.

SHIELD

O LORD, how many are my foes! How many rise up against me! Many are saying of me, "God will not deliver him." But you are a shield around me, O LORD; you bestow glory on me and lift up my head.

—Psalm 3:1-3 NIV

WHAT AN ENCOURAGING verse! Do you ever feel like you are surrounded on every side by people who are against you or don't care about you? I feel like that a lot. I first started feeling that way after my daughter was born and I moved back home. I know my family loved me, but I didn't feel like they liked me or cared about me very much. I felt so alone.

Now as an adult trying to follow Jesus and the plan he has for my life, I often feel resistance from everyone and everything around me. The writer of this psalm felt the same way. David was the king of the land, but his son Absalom wanted the kingdom for himself. He undercut David's rule, had himself pronounced king and sought to destroy the old regime, including his own father. Talk about resistance! David's own son was trying to kill him.

David was close to God. In fact, God called him "a man after my own heart." David enjoyed a close walk with God and knew how to rely on God in times of trouble. Earlier in David's life, then-king Saul was trying to kill him. David spent years running and hiding, sometimes in caves, from the king. But when given the opportunity to destroy the man who wanted to kill him, David trusted God and did not touch Saul in a violent way. That must have been hard for David because there were times when he could have killed Saul in his sleep. Saul's death would have been 'justified' since he was trying to kill David. Instead, David waited on God and trusted him for safety.

Does this describe you today? Do you trust God to take care of your enemies for you? Or at the first opportunity do you undermine their authority or talk about them behind their backs? Do you believe God has your best interests at heart? Do you believe he can take care of any situation, even the one you are in right now?

Spend some time asking God to be the Lord over your every circumstance. Trust him to provide what you need when you need it.

IN GOD'S IMAGE

When I consider your heavens, the work of your fingers, the moon and the stars, which you have set in place, what is man that you are mindful of him, the son of man that you care for him? You made him a little lower than the heavenly beings and crowned him with glory and honor. You made him ruler over the works of your hands; you put everything under his feet…"

—Psalm 8:3-6 NIV

DAVID STARTS AND ends this psalm by saying, "O Lord, our Lord, how majestic is your name in all the earth!" Like many of the Psalms, this one has been turned into a worship chorus that is sung in many churches. This song in particular has specific meaning to me. When I was pregnant, I lived at a maternity home on a large Christian compound. The church service every Sunday morning was broadcast throughout the compound as well as around the country. This song was used to open each and every Sunday service. The team would get the signal to begin, and then the band and praise team would start singing this song.

We like to look up at the stars at night and admire the handiwork. We like to find the constellations and name them. We launch rockets to explore the moon and the planets. God created the heavens and the earth. He named each star and then put it in its place. Nothing we see in the sky or on our planet is random. While some like to argue different theories, the truth is that God created it all. We have what we have because God has created it and given it to us.

God created humans in his own image. That doesn't mean we look like him physically, but boy do we resemble him spiritually! He made us like him. We have emotions, discernment, and the ability to learn and grow. Because of our sinful nature introduced in the Garden of Eden, we will never be perfect like him. In fact, we will never be perfect this side of heaven. That's why we need God. He cleanses us and covers us with his own perfection because we are not able to achieve that on our own. We are the crowning achievement of all of creation. In the six days it took God to create everything, we were saved until last. We are the only creatures made in his image.

Do you feel like you were made in God's image? Most days, neither do I. But you are. You are beautiful and special and created by God for his pleasure. You were made in the image of God. Take a few minutes and just enjoy that thought. Thank God for creating you and ask him to guide your every step so that you may bring glory to your creator.

THE FOOL

The fool says in his heart, "There is no God."

—Psalm 14:1 NIV

WEBSTER DEFINES A "fool" as *one who is deficient in judgment, sense, or understanding.* According to the above verse, the Bible defines a fool as an atheist, someone who is without God, and someone who doesn't believe in the existence of God.

Have you ever known anyone like this? Maybe you are one of these people. Maybe you are mad at God because of what has happened in your life. Or you are displeased with where your life is going or where it has been. Maybe you think you got the short end of the stick when you became part of the family you are in right now. Perhaps you want a newer car, a nicer house, or a better-paying job. Or you want a different husband or nicer kids. For any of these reasons, your heart may have become bitter toward God. And for that reason, you have turned away from God. Now you are trying to tell yourself that God doesn't exist because you are not happy with your life.

Living in denial doesn't make the truth go away. I can deny the existence of bugs in my yard and go out without any insect repellant on. But just because I don't believe the bugs are there doesn't stop me from coming inside with bites up and down my legs. Just because you don't believe in gravity and you jump off a building doesn't mean you won't get hurt or die. Denying the truth doesn't make it go away.

I think you get what I'm saying. My suggestion is to ask God to reveal himself to you. He created you and knows you better than anyone. Therefore, he knows how to speak to you in a way you can hear and understand. Keep a journal of your prayers to God and how he answers you in unique, specific ways. Be willing to think outside the box when it comes to this exercise. Remember that God can use anything or anyone, anywhere at any time to take care of your deepest need. It doesn't have to be a priest in a church or even someone who calls himself Christian. I think many people don't believe in God because they have never recognized his work in their lives. Be observant and ready to thank God at any moment for hearing you and responding to you.

Finally, prepare yourself to be amazed! I think I get so used to God blessing me that I don't always recognize it and give thanks for it right away. But on the days when I am really looking for God to reveal himself to me I am never left wondering. The way he takes care of my every need before I can even say it out loud is amazing! Who else created us and knows how to care for us like that? No one.

Take a minute and talk to God about these things. He's waiting on you to make the next move.

MY KNIGHT

I love you, GOD—you make me strong. GOD is bedrock under my feet, the castle in which I live, my rescuing knight. My God—the high crag where I run for dear life, hiding behind the boulders, safe in the granite hideout. I sing to GOD, the Praise-Lofty, and find myself safe and saved.

—Psalm 18:1-3

THE BOOK OF Psalms is lengthy—150 chapters—and is filled with songs of joy, sadness, sorrow, crying out, and you name it, it's in there. David wrote many of the psalms. He was a musician and lyricist before he was king. He loved music and loved to express himself through music. Even after he became king, David would sing and dance in public before the Lord to express his praise.

The way some of us best express our affection to God is through singing about him and to him. We find ourselves "at one" with much of the music and lyrics we hear in church and in the world. For those of us who are musical, we have to be careful what we listen to and what is going into our hearts and souls. For others of us, we best express our hearts to God through our moral lifestyle and our excellence at work.

David wrote psalms about everything. He took whatever was happening in his life to God. In this particular passage, David is once again thanking God for delivering him from the hands of his enemies. Although anointed by God for kingship and leadership of the people, he suffered much persecution from friends and enemies alike. There are plenty of other psalms that express those feelings. But this one in particular is thanking God for protecting him in times of danger.

In these verses, David expresses his love for God and then thanks him specifically. He tells God that he has been a strong place to stand and face the opposition. Then he calls him his rescuing knight. What an awesome picture of romance and bravery this is! It reminds me of the story of Rapunzel, trapped in the tall tower. At the same time God is David's saving knight, he is also David's mighty tower, protecting him from harm and from the elements. God is keeping him safe and is also his savior.

Can you say these things about God today? Is he your rescuing knight? Do you believe that God would do anything for you because he loves you? Take a minute now to reflect on this in your journal. Write your own psalm of praise to God for all he is and all he has done for you.

CHAMELEON

To the faithful you show yourself faithful, to the blameless you show yourself blameless, to the pure you show yourself pure, but to the crooked you show yourself shrewd. You save the humble but bring low those whose eyes are haughty.

—Psalm 18:25-27 NIV

HAVE YOU EVER noticed yourself sometimes acting differently depending on the situation? Perhaps at a party you act social, when you're really not that way in other areas of your life. At church you may act spiritual, while you may not behave that same way at home or school or work. Does this describe you in any way? I used to be good at being a chameleon, someone who just blends in with everyone else. After all, we want to be accepted. What better way is there than to go along with what the group already finds cool or fun or okay.

Books about men and women highlight these differences. We women have been compared to spaghetti, where all of our thoughts, hopes, experiences, and feelings are connected. Men, on the other hand, have been compared to waffles because of the individual squares on the top and bottom. These books claim that men can only operate in one box at a time; they can be chatty, or they can work, or they can be driving, but they can't do two or more of those things at the same time.

So, is this passage saying that God is unable to show more than one side of his personality at a time? Not exactly. God is good. God is *always* good. Depending on where we are in our faith walk with God, we may or may not believe this. But God responds to us in kind. If we are faithful and loving and make good choices, he responds to us favorably. Since the way we show our love and devotion to him is through obedience, he rewards and honors that. If our hearts are right before God, he has no need to correct us.

But woe to the man who acts against God, who does what he does in the name of God but without the heart attitude of God. This is where we get into false religions and teachings, including cults and secular humanism. These groups say they believe in God and act in the name of God, but their hearts are far from God. The truth is, they don't have Jesus in their hearts.

What does this mean to us? In a world as cold and hard as ours, who wouldn't want to live in the land of God's favor? Walking closely with God is as good as it's going to get this side of heaven. Do you know God today? Have you received him into your heart and life? Are you acting out of love and devotion to him or out of your own nature? Take a minute and reflect on this. Ask God to help you live for him out of love and devotion.

THE MARK OF
THE CREATOR

The heavens declare the glory of God; the skies proclaim the work of his hands. Day after day they pour forth speech; night after night they display knowledge.

—Psalm 19:1-2 NIV

I HEARD A story recently about Helen Keller. As soon as her teacher taught her sign language, her teacher told her about God. Helen Keller said she always knew there had to be a God even though she couldn't hear or see. How is that possible?

I believe that created things bear the marks of their creator. Artists' drawings bear certain artistic earmarks. Maybe it's the way the eyes are slanted or the way the wrinkles curve up on the ends. Maybe it's the color palette they tend to use. In the case of a carpenter or woodworker, they tend to have their favorite ways to finish a project. But the truth is a piece of work will bear the mark of its creator. Even if something is mass produced, there will still be evidence of *which* machine produced it.

What does this mean for us? God created each one of us *individually*. You are not the result of mass production or evolution spanning millions of years. You are fearfully and wonderfully made. We are all special and unique in our own ways. Don't believe in God? It doesn't matter. Not believing in him doesn't make him go away. You are still created by him for his pleasure. We bear the mark of our creator.

Some people say we have a God-shaped vacuum inside each of us. While we may try to fill it with relationships or things or money, the only thing that truly fits is a relationship with Jesus Christ. I have also heard some people say that they don't have that vacuum. I'm not sure I believe that. We bear the mark of our creator, but what does that look like?

Jesus was a living, breathing human being. He cried, he laughed, he had friends, he enjoyed being with his friends and family, he traveled, he had compassion for others. Are we not like him in those ways? He loved to heal the sick, teach others, and care for orphans. Does that not sound like a doctor or teacher or social worker? We are not all the same, but we all bear his mark.

The skies and the stars are also part of God's creation. They too bear the mark of their creator. In their own way, they express that uniqueness and the hand that made them. They are a witness to the universe that there *is* a God, just like Helen Keller knew before she could communicate. Is there evidence of God in your life today? What is it? Take a minute to reflect on how you resemble your creator.

OUR HOPE IS
IN THE LORD

Now I know that the LORD saves his anointed; he answers him from his holy heaven with the saving power of his right hand. Some trust in chariots and some in horses, but we trust in the name of the LORD our God.

—Psalm 20:6-7 NIV

THIS WAS OBVIOUSLY written for a king who had an army and chariots and horses. It was written by David—who wrote many of the Psalms—just as the army was going out on a mission. Before each mission, the king and the armies would pray for victory over the enemy. They would renew their faith and trust in God as provider and victor.

We've all heard of foxhole prayers, those prayers uttered by a soldier as he is holed up during combat. This may have been similar, although in those days, the armies had a great faith in God, which was encouraged by their continuing victories.

This can get confusing if you are new to a relationship with God. I'm not saying that the armed services do not have faith in God now, so don't misinterpret. I'm pointing out that in those days, faith was a very common thing to express out in the open.

No doubt this army was very successful, which bolstered their faith in God. But the truth of the matter is that we cannot base our view of God on our own circumstances and surroundings. Those soldiers didn't love God because they were successful, they just loved him because he's

God. It's easy to love God and praise him when all is going well. But what happens when you lose your job, family, or loved one? That's when the true test of our faith really begins.

By declaring that other armies may put their confidence in their state-of-the-art chariots, purebred horses, or expert marksmen, this army put all of their trust and hope and faith in the one true God. Nothing else. No one else. They were trained and kept their equipment serviced and in good running order, but that is not what they put their assurance in.

Have you put all your eggs in one basket? Or are you still trusting in your own abilities and gifts and talents? Are you merely giving lip-service to God while continuing to live life your own way on your own terms? Take a minute and reflect on which "army" you fall into. Ask God to help you become more like him.

FORGIVEN

Show me your ways, O LORD, teach me your paths; Remember not the sins of my youth and my rebellious ways; according to your love remember me, for you are good, O LORD.

—Psalm 25:4,7 NIV

IF YOU HAVE been a Christian for very long, you are familiar with God's forgiveness. It's one of his hallmarks, one of the things everyone talks about. He is always loving and always forgiving, no matter what. It doesn't matter what you've done or where you've been, God is waiting for you to ask him to forgive you. Why? He's already paid the penalty for every sin you have committed and will ever commit. When he died on the cross, he took on your past, present, and future sins just like he did for me and for every other person who has lived in the past, is living now, and will ever live.

I often wonder if forgiving the sins I commit every day is hard for God. I doubt it. He's in the business of forgiveness, right? But I sometimes think it's harder for me to ask forgiveness for certain things because that would mean I have to admit them to myself. Does that make sense? The word is denial. Since our nature is to sin and to do it often, it's easy to overlook things we do in our life that are actually sin. I get complacent and just assume God will forgive me without asking him to. But God wants me to ask. He wants me to admit that I need him and that I cannot do it on my own.

In this passage, I wonder what David was thinking. It seems to me that he continues to be grieved by things he did a long time ago in his youth. Can you relate? I certainly can. I have made so many bad choices in my life. Having sex with my high-school boyfriend was just the beginning. It was downhill from there. The more bad decisions I made, the worse I felt about myself, so the more bad choices I made… and so on. Some of those choices have haunted me, especially since I became a Christian. Forgiving myself has been the big challenge. God forgave me the minute I asked him.

The good news is that if you are a believer and have received Jesus Christ into your heart and life, then the only thing he sees when he looks at you is the blood that was shed when he died on the cross for you. His blood covers every sin and stain in your past, present, and future life. He desires for you to learn and grow and be a new creature, different from who you were in the past. But obviously we can't make our past mistakes un-happen. All we can do is walk with God in a new way. And it's never too late to start. Won't you say "yes" to him today and say "no" to your former way of life? Let him lead you and guide you and show you the new life he has in store for you. He's just waiting for you to ask.

Take a minute and reflect. Where are you in your journey? Where would you like to be? Ask God to show you a new way.

THE LORD IS
MY SHEPHERD

Even though I walk through the valley of the shadow of death, I
will fear no evil, for you are with me; your rod and your staff, they
comfort me.

—Psalm 23:4 NIV

WHILE THIS SOUNDS wonderful, God's presence may not
seem like much if you truly are in the valley. Are you there today?
I have spent many days and months and years trapped in the "valley
of the shadow of death." I wanted to die. Surely death would be easier
than what I was dealing with. Grief. Loss. Despair. Loneliness like I
didn't know existed. Hopeless that it was ever going to get better. Not
a friend in the world to talk to outside of hand-written letters to friends
who were so far away they might as well have been on another planet.

I knew God was watching over me, seeing me and knowing what
was going on in my head. I knew he longed to embrace me and have
me know the depths of his love for me. I knew his angels prayed over
me and for me because I surely didn't know how to pray or what to
pray for. And I knew he was patiently waiting for me to come to him
and ask, "Is this all there is?"

I'm a slow learner, so it took me a long time to get to that place. I
knew there had to be more to life than sadness and darkness. I wanted
there to be more to life than those things. I think the first major break-
through came about six years after Katie was born. It was Father's Day

weekend and I was living in Florida for the summer with some college friends. I was to graduate that December, and this was no vacation (I had a job), but it was certainly fun. I was sitting in church on that Sunday, when out of nowhere I heard a voice in my head say, *Forgive him.* Like a ton of bricks the overwhelming need to forgive Katie's birth father hit me. It was unnerving. I shook and cried and prayed. And prayed. And prayed some more. At the end of that prayer I felt something new and different: FREEDOM!

In this passage, I usually focus on the valley-of-death part. It's dark and gloomy and depressing. But the commentary related to this passage reminds us that it's the valley of the *shadow* of death. Think about your shadow. It has no power. It can't hurt you. It may look like you, but it's not you.

Just like the shadow of death. It can't hurt you. It can only lurk around the corner and really creep you out. It can scare you, *but it can't hurt you.* Wherever you are today, God is there. He is with you and near you. All you have to do is take one step toward him. Ask him to reveal himself in your life. You are not alone.

Take a minute and write in your journal all that's in your heart right now. Thank God that he loves you and is always available to you.

HOW IT IS

The earth is the LORD's, and everything in it, the world, and all who live in it; for he founded it upon the seas and established it upon the waters...

—Psalm 24:1-2 NIV

OUR SCHOOLS AND education system are filled with different theories about how the world came into being. Some say a big explosion took place and the solar system is what is left over. Some say humans have evolved over thousands of years. The Bible says that God created the heavens and the earth. This passage alludes to the fact that God created the world from the bottom up, that he started with the seas and went from there.

If God started with the ocean and the waves and the sand, do you think he's able to create trees and flowers? What about mountains and snow? If you truly believe that God created everything, doesn't that mean that everything belongs to God? And if God owns everything, what does that mean to you and your life?

I remember learning in elementary school about the Native Americans and how the white man learned to trade with them. They used ropes and shells to buy food and grain. Whose idea do you think it was to trade something for goods and services? Isn't that the foundation for our system of money today? But since God created the people and the goods and the services, doesn't that mean that money was his idea? Don't you think that God knew there would be a need for money?

Here's my point: If God is the creator of everything in the whole universe, doesn't that mean that everything belongs to him? I think we can get so caught up in our stuff and our money that we forget that *we don't own it.* Everything we have belongs to God; he merely entrusts it to us while we are alive. Everything we have—from our car to the money in the bank—is a test to see how we will manage it and if we will honor God with it. God is interested in our heart attitude, and that is evidenced by how we spend our time, what we do with how God made us, and what we do with our material and financial resources.

Giving money to our local church or charity or giving away things we no longer use doesn't seem to be such a big deal in the light of that truth, does it? God wants us to hold on loosely to the things in our lives. He doesn't want us to get so caught up in our stuff and our money that we lose sight of what is most important, which is our family, our relationships with others, and our relationship with God.

Take a minute to reflect right now on where you are with your stuff. How important is money to you? More important than your relationships? More important than your family? More important than God? The Bible says that anything that comes between us and God is an idol. Is money your idol?

MY CONFIDENCE

The LORD is my light and my salvation—whom shall I fear? The LORD is the stronghold of my life—of whom shall I be afraid? When evil men advance against me to devour my flesh, when my enemies and my foes attack me, they will stumble and fall. Though an army besiege me, my heart will not fear; though war break out against me, even then will I be confident.

—Psalm 27:1-3 NIV

THIS IS MY "confidence" passage of the Bible. Whenever I am feeling overcome or attacked or ganged up on (anyone ever feel like that?), this is where I turn. I believe God has a plan and a purpose for my life. I believe that he chooses humans to carry out his plans, despite how inept and sinful we are. I have tried my hardest to mess up my life, but God continues to forgive me and use me anyway.

I often feel that I am one bad decision away from slipping out of God's grasp. I know that is not entirely true, but for me, my faith is paramount to my daily life. I spend time in the Bible and in prayer daily because I don't want to lose the ground God has gained in my life. I spent many years living my own way and acting as if I was in charge, and those were years wasted. *I was a Christian then.* I knew God, but I chose to live contrary to that commitment. I can remember the spot on the interstate where God spoke to me plainly, in an audible voice. He told me that I needed to make a choice, but the way I was living was hypocritical. It made me catch my breath because in my mind, hypocrites were the worst.

Now that I'm right with God, he is my defense. He fights my battles. He protects me and guides me. I'm no puppet, believe me. God gave us free will, and he will never mess with that. I am stubborn and strong-willed and oftentimes try to take things into my own hands and do them my own way. But it doesn't take me as long now to ask him for help or for forgiveness (which happens often). We can run away all we want, but God is only one step away from us.

Where are you today in your relationship with God? Are you honoring your commitment to him? Or do you have yet to make that kind of commitment to him? Take a minute and ask God to make it plain to you where you stand with him. Ask him what you need to do to walk more closely with him.

EXTREME GOD

Blessed be GOD—he heard me praying. He proved he's on my side;
I've thrown my lot in with him.

—Psalm 28:6-7

D O YOU LIKE extreme sports? Do you like to bungee jump or
skydive? What about rappelling or mountain climbing? All these
sports have something important in common. While you may be thinking adrenaline is the common factor, I'm thinking something more on
the spiritual side. It takes faith to jump out of an airplane and believe
the parachute will open. It takes faith to believe that a human-sized
rubber band is strong enough to keep you from falling to the elements
below. Faith is stepping out to do something that is fun and dangerous
while believing that you are going to live through it. Faith in Jesus is
no different. In fact, I believe faith in God to be the most exhilarating,
death-defying activity I've ever undertaken.

How do we know when we have taken that step to put our entire
trust in God? For me, it always feels like stepping off a cliff. I've done
everything I can humanly do. I have done the homework, the research,
the praying, the talking to the experts, the emotional preparation. But
faith is actually a verb; faith is in the *doing*. After all I can humanly do is
said and done, faith is stepping out and not knowing what will happen
next, but believing that God is in control. Faith is putting all your eggs
in one basket, so to speak, and not relying on yourself or anyone else,

but solely on God to provide what you need when you need it. Faith does not know what is needed, but it is trusting God to show up and provide just the right thing at just the right time.

I heard a story recently that illustrates faith and belief. Belief is having confidence in something. So I can have confidence in the fact that an elevator is going to carry me to the top of a building. I can review the engineering for myself and believe the building is sound. I can look at the cables that carry the elevator and see that they are in good shape. I can inspect the elevator car with my own eyes and see that it is intact. I can believe the elevator will take me to the top of the building with all my heart and mind. But my believing all this will happen isn't enough; belief alone will not get me to the top of the building. Faith is getting into the elevator.

Where are you today? God created you and wants to do great things in you and through you. But in the process, you will need to step out in faith and allow him to do those things in your life. Are you willing to do that today? Take a minute and ask God to build your faith and to give you opportunities to do that.

CONFESSION IS GOOD FOR THE SOUL

When I kept silent, my bones wasted away through my groaning all day long. For day and night your hand was heavy upon me; my strength was sapped as in the heat of summer. Then I acknowledged my sin to you and did not cover up my iniquity. I said, "I will confess my transgressions to the LORD"—and you forgave the guilt of my sin.

—Psalm 32:3-5 NIV

ENVY. RAGE. JEALOUSY. Bitterness. Anger. Addiction. Anxiety. Which of these describes you right now? Maybe you are dealing with more than one. Maybe there's something going on with you that isn't listed. All of these things have something in common. Do you have any idea what it is?

All of these things go against God and his nature. God is pure and holy. We don't really understand what that is anymore, but if you have ever been around very small children, they can give you an idea. A sleeping child looks so pure and innocent. Even after a horrible day filled with tantrums and tears, there is something so peaceful and almost holy about watching a child sleep.

Unlike a child, God is wise and holy. But that picture of a small child gives you an idea of what holiness looks like. God calls us to be holy because he is holy. He doesn't want us to be naïve like a child. He wants us to be wholly devoted to him and not steeped in the junk of the world.

This passage talks about being oppressed by the sin in our lives. We are spiritual beings by nature. If we continue going on our way, living our life the way we want to and forgetting about God, it will catch up with us. This passage leaves us wondering how far the root of our sin goes. For example, is it possible that the root cause of depression is sin? How about the root cause of anxiety or an eating disorder? What about adultery? If we were right with God to begin with, would the person we were not married to be all that attractive to us?

David gives us a picture here that makes me think of a very depressed person. Bones were wasting away. Groaning. Sapped strength. That sounds like me when I'm depressed. But then David acknowledges his sin to God and he's better. Isn't that interesting? If God created us and knows us, doesn't he already know about our sin? Do we really have to tell him about it? Well, he wants to hear it from us. Yes he knows what we have done, but he wants us to tell him that *we* know what we have done.

Take a minute and think about where you are right now. Is something plaguing you, and you can't figure out why? Ask God to reveal any unconfessed sin in your life. Ask him to give you the courage and strength necessary to recognize it and confess it.

GETTING WHAT I WANT

> Delight yourself in the LORD and he will give you the desires of your heart.
>
> —Psalm 37:4 NIV

FINALLY! A VERSE that talks about something we all care about: getting what we want. What is the deepest desire of your heart? What are you really working for in this life? I have a friend who describes her job as a way to fund her real passion. Does that describe you? Or are you fortunate enough to work in a field you are passionate about and get paid for it?

I went through a time in my life when I knew God wanted me to work at a particular place. I was excited because this particular clinic was world-renowned for its cutting-edge treatment. People would literally fly in from all over the world just to stay and receive services from this place. I thought it was a dream come true. In fact, I thought this was God giving me the desire of my heart. After all, that's what the above verse says, isn't it? Unfortunately for me, I had disregarded the first part of the verse. God gives us the desires of our heart *after* we delight ourselves in him. What does that mean?

Webster defines "delight" as *to give great pleasure, satisfaction, or enjoyment; to please highly.* According to the verse, the way we delight ourselves in God is to please him. How do we do that? The Bible says that our God created us for his own enjoyment. Just the fact that you

125

exist brings a smile to God's face. Did you know that? He created you special and unlike anyone else for his own good pleasure. We please God when we love him with all of our hearts, all of our souls, all of our minds, and all of our bodies. When we desire to serve him and live for him above everything and everyone else, that's when we are giving him great pleasure.

I wasn't delighting myself in God at that time in my life. I was pretty much delighting myself in myself, actually. I wanted what I wanted regardless of what God or anyone else had to say about it. We have to be right with God before he can bless us. And giving us the desires of our heart is a huge blessing.

So why didn't God want me to have what I wanted? First of all, I'm not sure that's the right question. It's not that he didn't want me to have what I wanted. It's that I didn't *know* what I wanted. God wants to give us the desires of our heart *after* we delight ourselves in him. The process of getting right with God and delighting ourselves in him *often changes our heart's desires*. I know it sounds crazy. But I challenge you to get right with God before assessing what your heart's desire is. *Getting right with God means that my desires are replaced with God's desires.* So it turns out my heart's desire wasn't to work at that clinic. My true heart's desire was to write this for you.

Take a minute and ask God to show you his desire for your life.

THE DEER

As the deer pants for streams of water, so my soul pants for you, O God. My soul thirsts for God, for the living God. When can I go and meet with God? My tears have been my food day and night…

—Psalm 42:1-3 NIV

PLANTS AREN'T MY thing. Some people have green thumbs. I think mine is black. When I first got married, my new husband's home was full of beautiful green, leafy plants and trees. Ten years later, I still struggle to keep one little leafy plant alive. Usually I forget to water, so the plant shrivels up and dies. Either that or I remember to water all the time, and the plant drowns. Plants aren't my thing.

But under my husband's direction, I was watering our outside flower barrels this morning. As I watched, I noticed the water from the shower nozzle make its way to the root of the plant. This one plant in particular, affectionately called a spikey thing, was fascinating. I watched as the drops of water followed a path through the center of the leaf to get to the root. The spikey leaf was purposefully engineered to deliver the life-giving water where it was needed the most: the roots. I was transfixed as I watched drop after drop flow quickly down the leaf to the root.

Oddly enough, I saw myself in that plant. My soul needs to be watered. I need something deeper than church once a week. I need something more than drive-thru spirituality. What about you? I have friends and hobbies. I like to eat and play and shop, in that order. But those things don't feed my soul. Those things don't go down deep and keep me going today and tomorrow and the next day. I need more. I need more than what the world is offering. I need more than fashionable clothing and cool hair and perfect skin. I need more than last week's church service to keep me walking through this sad/hard/frustrating day I'm having. What about you? Are you there?

I don't know where you're at or what you're dealing with, but I know the answer. Jesus is the answer to every question you have. God is the answer to every trial, to every hurt. The Bible is the answer to every injustice, every situation you are facing. The God of Christianity is not one that was carved out of wood or stone. This God is a man who walked on this earth, lived in our skin, and experienced every situation possible. He is your answer.

Do you trust him today? If you have not done so already, admit now that you are a sinner, that you believe that Jesus is Lord and you want him to come into your heart and change your life. If you are already a Christian, ask God to water your weary soul. Ask him to encourage you. Water your soul each day by spending time reading the Bible and praying. Get involved in church beyond Sunday morning attendance. Find a small group of women who meet regularly to discuss relevant Bible topics. If you actively pursue God, he will actively pursue you.

9/11

God is our refuge and strength, an ever-present help in trouble. Therefore we will not fear, though the earth give way and the mountains fall into the heart of the sea, though its waters roar and foam and the mountains quake with their surging.

—Psalm 46:1-3 NIV

I'LL NEVER FORGET the morning of September 11, 2001. I was in Jazzercise class, as usual, and when I got into my car afterwards, I flipped on the radio. I was initially annoyed at hearing Peter Jennings' voice instead of music. After a good workout I am energized and ready to get my day going. I didn't want to listen to some dumb news report; I wanted to turn up the music! But every station I turned to, it was the same thing. It then dawned on me that something newsworthy might be going on and maybe I should pay attention. I heard the words Mr. Jennings was saying, but I didn't understand. I couldn't wrap my mind around the picture he was painting.

I grew up on the east coast. I loved New York City as a kid. I loved the skyscrapers, the smell of pollution, walking around downtown, going to the theatre. I was a dancer in my younger years, and NYC was the Mecca of all that was dance. I loved the thrill of the live theatre, where anything could happen at any time. My first musical ever was *A Chorus Line* when it was on Broadway the first time. Looking back, that seems like kind of a racy show for such a young girl! My mom, sister, grandmom, and I—and whatever friends we could pile in the car—spent many happy weekends making the drive to and from the city. What a thrill! I can remember the first time we went to Ellis Island and climbed to the top of the Statue of Liberty. I think I was in a lot better shape then. We would go to Macy's at Christmas time and get lost in the winter wonderland they would create. Amazing memories that formed who I was as a child.

That's why on the morning of September 11, I just could not understand what was being said. I'm sure he was speaking English. I understood the individual words he was using, but together they made no sense. Airplanes in buildings? What was that?

I sat in my driveway with my mouth hanging open as Mr. Jennings' voice cracked and went silent when he announced the collapse of the first tower. What was happening? And where was God in all of this? I remember walking around my house the rest of that day, afraid the ceiling was going to fall down on top of me.

That's what these verses are about. Our God is as solid as a rock. He never moves. He never changes. He never sleeps. And he is never, *ever* caught unaware. The part of this verse that says "though the mountains fall into the heart of the sea"…that's where I was that sad morning. Although the "mountains" were man-made, they had been a symbol of this country for decades. And now they were gone. But guess what? Our God is as firm and as faithful and as loving as ever.

Are your feet planted on the solid rock of Christ? Will you be ready when the next disaster or crisis hits? Take a minute now and get right with the God who created you.

KEEPING UP WITH
THE JONESES

So don't be impressed with those who get rich and pile up fame and fortune. They can't take it with them; fame and fortune all get left behind. Just when they think they've arrived and folks praise them because they've made good, they enter the family burial plot where they'll never see sunshine again. We aren't immortal. We don't last long. Like our dogs, we age and weaken. And die.

—Psalm 49:16-20

OFTEN WHEN I meet new people, I have to remind myself that they are no different from me. They get hungry and have to eat. They get tired and need to sleep. They get thirsty and have to drink. I try my hardest to look at people with spiritual eyes and to see beyond their exteriors. We all need God. It doesn't matter how rich, tall, educated, or gifted we are, we all need God.

But sometimes this is not so easy for me. I can get intimidated by a person's wealth of experience. Or their amazing education. Or their position. I recently invited an old friend to have lunch and mentor me on some of the finer points of nonprofit board management. This person has held various important positions in leadership, and I knew when I asked him that he would have some wise insights to share with me. However, as our lunch approached, I grew more and more nervous. My husband finally confronted me with my anxiety, and I blurted out, "But do you know who he is?" My husband just blinked and said, "Yes, he used to be in our Bible study." I had gotten myself all worked up over someone who—at the core of his being—is just a person, a Christian, a creation of our heavenly Father. All of those titles and experiences mean nothing to God.

Have you been here? Have you been in the place where you are afraid to speak, afraid to make yourself known to another? I think at the core of being human is the fear that if other people really knew who we were, really knew what we were like and what our private thoughts and motives were, we would not be esteemed, respected, or thought well of. We are consumed with what others think of us. The only person that matters is Jesus Christ. His opinion of us is the only thing that matters. Yes, he wants us to be above reproach and obedient. Yes, he wants us to be loving and kind and faithful. But at the base of our being we are all human and broken. We all struggle with sin even though it looks different to each of us.

We will all die one day. What do you want your legacy to be? What do you want others to remember about you? That you were completely consumed with your reputation? That you were completely consumed with living up to others' expectations of you? Or that you were completely sold out to God and willing to go where he sent you and do whatever he asked of you, even if you looked like a fool in the process. Think about it. Then ask God to show you what he wants from you.

COMPLETELY DEPENDABLE

Have mercy on me, O God, according to your unfailing love; according to your great compassion blot out my transgressions.

—Psalm 51:1 NIV

THOSE OF US who are in Christ are the lucky ones. Sure, our lives aren't easy and problem-free, but look at who we have as our advocate. This song was written by David, a young man whom God had anointed king. After years and years of following God, David had a moment of weakness and committed adultery. But look at his cry for forgiveness. He knows he has done wrong. He knows that he has sinned against God. He seeks immediately to restore his fellowship with God. He knows what he has lost, and he doesn't want it standing in the way of his relationship with God for one second longer.

The coolest thing about this verse is that David asks for God's mercy "according to *your* unfailing love." He doesn't ask God to reconcile with him on David's terms. He throws himself at the feet of God and begs him to use his own judgment in dealing with his sin.

According to Webster, "unfailing" means *completely dependable*. Let me ask you something. Are you completely dependable? Do you do everything you say you are going to do? Are you physically and mentally and spiritually and emotionally able to carry your own load and that of your friends and family on your own, every day, without fail? Do you ever get tired? Or lonely? Or depressed? If so, then you are not completely dependable.

We cannot do things on our own. We are not able. We were not created with this capacity. As humans we are weak, which is how God created us. If we were able to do all these things on our own, why would we need God? We wouldn't.

Fortunately for us, God is completely dependable. He doesn't get tired or hungry or thirsty or bored. He is not like us. He is completely faithful, all-knowing, all-wise, and all-seeing. He is also all-merciful. He holds the power of life and death in his hands. If we try and reconcile with God, we cannot do it in our own power. But if we humble ourselves and allow God to do the reconciling and the work, he will be more compassionate to us than we could ever imagine.

Do you trust him today? Do you trust him to be merciful to you even when you don't deserve it? Give it a try. Tell God of your failings and your shortcomings. Ask him to deal with you according to his unfailing love. You might be surprised at what happens.

DAVID'S HEART

Create in me a pure heart, O God, and renew a steadfast spirit within me. Do not cast me from your presence or take your Holy Spirit from me. Restore to me the joy of your salvation and grant me a willing spirit, to sustain me.

—Psalm 51:10-12 NIV

THIS SONG IS another example of David's writings to God. He loved God so much and enjoyed such a close companionship with him that he didn't want anything to get in his way. Webster defines "create" this way: *to cause to happen; bring about; arrange, as by intention or design*. Notice something about this. David did not ask God to clean up his heart because it was dirty. He didn't ask him to *restore* a pure heart in him. No, David asked God to *create* a pure heart in him. By definition we know that he was asking God to give him something he didn't already possess.

None of us has a pure heart. *Not one of us.* Not you. Not me. We are all born sinners. After Adam and Eve, none of us stands a chance. We have failed before we have even begun. We have all missed the boat, and there is no chance of us ever redeeming ourselves by being good enough or obedient enough.

Now that we're all on the same page, let's go on. Next, David asks God to "renew a steadfast spirit." Since he's asking God to restore this spirit within him and not create it, David must already have had that in

135

him at some time. David is asking God to restore an unwavering spirit in his heart. He is asking God to make him unmovable, unshakeable again.

Earlier in this same chapter David is seeking to reconcile with God because of his sin of adultery. But this passage seems to go a step further. Yes, David desires to be forgiven of his sin. Don't we all when we screw up? But for David, being forgiven wasn't enough. He sought restoration. Lucky for him that God is in the restoration business.

Did you know that there is no sin, no place on this earth where you are out of God's reach? No matter how far away from God you feel, he is only one step away. All you have to do is cry out to him and believe he hears you. His desire is for you to be reconciled to him. He deeply, passionately desires a relationship with you. He wishes to provide for your every need whether financial, emotional, or physical. If he had it his way, no one would perish without the knowledge of the saving grace of God. He not only desires a relationship with us, but he wants to restore us and our lives. He can literally give you back the years the locusts have eaten. His Word says it and I've seen it in my own life.

Won't you trust him today? Take a minute and ask God to create in you a pure heart and restore in you a faith that is unmovable, unshakeable.

MY SACRIFICE

You do not delight in sacrifice, or I would bring it; you do not take pleasure in burnt offerings. The sacrifices of God are a broken spirit; a broken and contrite heart, O God, you will not despise.

—Psalm 51:16-17 NIV

IF YOU'VE READ any part of the Old Testament, you've undoubtedly read about bulls, birds, goats, and other types of livestock being slaughtered and then burned on an altar as a sacrifice to God. It's hard to imagine what that really must have been like. When we read about it, everything sounds so nice and neat. But the reality of slaughtering one or a hundred bulls is bloody, messy, hard work. The message is clear: sacrificing is hard work.

Now, because we have Jesus who willingly sacrificed himself on a cross, we no longer need to slaughter animals and sacrifice them to God. No longer do we need to burn animals on an outdoor altar in order to make amends with God. The look of our sacrifice has changed. In some ways, maybe it was easier to cut up an animal and burn it. What God asks us to do today instead is far harder.

The sacrifice God wants to see in our lives happens on the inside; the old way of sacrifice was external. God is more concerned with the condition of our hearts than with any other single factor of our lives. He wants us to live whole, healthy lives, and that starts with our heart. Just like the major organs in our body depend on the heart to pump the blood, our spiritual life begins with the heart. We must be right with God. We must confess him as Lord. We must seek to follow him in all we do and say. Nothing else matters. We can say all the right things and do all the right things and look good on the outside. We can fool everyone around us, but we cannot fool God. If our hearts are not right with him, *nothing* else matters.

God desires all of us, and that starts with our hearts. Does he have your heart today? Take a few minutes and thank God that you belong to him. Haven't made that commitment yet? It's never too late. Ask God to come into your heart and life and make you new from the inside out.

THE ANT

You lazy fool, look at an ant. Watch it closely; let it teach you a thing or two. Nobody has to tell it what to do. All summer it stores up food; at harvest it stockpiles provisions. So how long are you going to laze around doing nothing? How long before you get out of bed?
—Proverbs 6:6-9

A LITTLE SLEEP, a little slumber, a little folding of your hands to rest, and scarcity and poverty will come upon you. That's the next part of this passage. Our world likes to say "God helps those who help themselves," but is that really true? Is that really how God works?

Look at the passage. God has given the ant strength for its tasks, wisdom to know when to store up food, and knowledge to do its task within the time allotted. Because the ant works hard all summer, it gets to eat all winter. Because the ant is not lazy, it is provided for. These little creatures are all drones, except for the queen. She leads them on their tasks, hurries them along and then tells them when their work is done and it's time to rest. Ants are simple creatures. They work. They eat. Then they die. Maybe we've made life too complicated.

God has enabled and empowered the ant to do what is necessary when it's necessary. I'm not sure about God helping the ants because they help themselves, but I do know God created the ant to be mindful of him. His apparent promise to the ants is that if they work hard, he will make sure they are fed.

So, if God cares that much about an ant, how much more do you think he cares about you and me? Can it really be that simple? If we listen to God and are mindful of him at every turn, don't you think he will care for us? Don't you think he will feed us and clothe us and shelter us?

Let me ask you a question. What would happen if you just shut out the world and its influences, pressures, and priorities and just focused on God for the next thirty days? What would happen if you gave God full reign in your professional life, your personal life, and your social life? What if you gave him free reign over what you watched on television and listened to on the radio? What if you sought his advice on who you spent time with and what you talked about? Just think about it. How different would your life be? How different *could* it be?

The Bible promises that if we seek God with all of our heart we will find him. He can care for you. He can provide for all of your needs. Just trust him today.

THE BALANCE

Roll your works upon the Lord [commit and trust them wholly to Him; He will cause your thoughts to become agreeable to His will, and] so shall your plans be established and succeed.

—Proverbs 16:3 AMP

ONE OF THE confusing things in learning to walk with God and having a relationship with him is figuring out where he fits into our lives. In our old way of life, we did and thought and planned all by ourselves. We filled out our calendars according to what we wanted and needed to do. We planned our vacations according to where we wanted to go. It was all about us. Everything in our lives was about us.

But now we're Christians and we know something is different. Something has changed. But our brains are used to doing some things a certain way because we have been doing things that same way for a long time. One of those things is our time and our schedule and our calendar. We are used to making all of the decisions about our life and then letting others know as needed. As Christians, God wants us to build our lives around *him*. Even our schedules. Even our calendars. Even our vacations.

How do we do that? How do we make the shift from what we want to do with our time to figuring out what God wants to do with our time while still getting our chores and responsibilities done?

I think prayer is the key. We can't hear from God if we don't have open communication with him. Obviously there are certain things we have to do at certain times. We have to go to work. We have to keep our appointments. These things are God-honoring in their nature. Then we pray about what to do with the rest of our time. We ask God at the beginning of the day, the week, or the month to show us how to use our time. We ask and then watch for him to show us, to give us opportunities to honor him.

As I write this, I'm having a really bad hair day. It is tempting for me to spend the time my daughter is in school to get a haircut and color and make myself feel better. But the reality is that we have limited time, and sometimes we have to choose between good and best. Spending this time writing is far more honoring to God than spending time obsessing over my hair. Not that looking good is bad. But we need to find a balance.

I challenge you to write down in a notebook how much time each day you spend in your various activities. Do this for one week. Use that list to guide you in praying specifically over things you are involved in. Ask God to show you anything that should come off that list. Ask him to show you if there's something that you are not doing that he would have you do. Ask him to make it very clear to you.

WOUNDS FROM
A FRIEND

> If an enemy were insulting me, I could endure it; if a foe were raising himself against me, I could hide from him. But it is you, a man like myself, my companion, my close friend, with whom I once enjoyed sweet fellowship as we walked with the throng at the house of God.
> —Psalm 55:12-14 NIV

*O*UCH. WHO WANTS to read this passage, let alone write about it? The painful reality is that the church is full of humans, some of whom have been forgiven and set free by Jesus. The truth is that we all continue to fall short of perfection; far, far short. How many of us have been hurt the most by Christians, people professing to be born-again, washed-in-the-blood, salt-of-the-earth believers in Christ? We can expect people who don't know God to hurt us. In fact, we should expect it. But to whom much is given, much is required, right? So we expect people who claim to be Christians to maintain a much higher standard.

The problem here is not that people do stupid things. It's that we have a different set of expectations for different groups of people. People are people. Yes, God is big and powerful, but he will never mess with our free will and our decisions to act out of our humanness instead of out of his strength.

Like you, I've experienced a deep hurt from someone I thought was a true friend. We were friends for years after having met at church. We were in a small group together. We spent time together. I really thought

I knew her. Then she said words that cut me to the core and made me wonder if we were really friends at all. It took me a while to understand what could make one friend say such stupid, selfish, hurtful words to another friend. But I let God have it and he healed my wound. The friendship, however, was over.

That was many years ago. But here's the kicker. She has become even more successful than she was. I have struggled with that. I have struggled with the notion that God has rewarded her for her unloving words toward me. And I had to start praying about it again, even after years had passed.

This is what God told me. God's will is not stopped. It will not be changed or blocked, no matter what our choices. God's will keeps moving forward, and sometimes we are blessed to be able to join in the work with him. Her success has nothing to do with me and everything to do with God. He is doing a work in her life despite her wrong choices or hurtful words. My part is not to hold her to a certain standard because she calls herself a Christian, but to see her as God sees her and extend even more grace to her *because* she is a Christian.

Have you been hurt by a close friend? A brother or sister in Christ? Ask God to show you what hurt you still hold in your heart and help you forgive. Ask God to restore your hurting heart.

HOPE

There is surely a future hope for you, and your hope will not be cut off.

—Proverbs 23:18 NIV

WHAT IS THE hope you have for your child? For me it was that she would have a better life than I could give her. A life with two parents and opportunities for education. I was not equipped to give my child those things. So my hope has always been not that she would have a perfect life, but that she would have more opportunities than I could have provided for her.

Abortion ends the possibility of hope, literally cuts it off. That is not a judgment; that is truth. But adoption gives kids a hope unlike anything else. No matter what that child was born out of—rape, incest, poor choices—that doesn't have to be their legacy. They can start over with a clean slate. That's what adoption does.

What were your reasons for choosing adoption? How are you with that decision right now, today? Our predicament is a weird one, for sure. We endure all the hardships with none of the rewards. We have sacrificed our bodies, our lifestyles, and our lives only to come home empty-handed. Our reward is knowing our child is alive and safe and being taken care of in a way that we were not able to provide for them.

The weird part comes from going through a grieving process when we haven't physically lost someone. If a friend or family member dies, we grieve for them because they aren't there anymore. But our children *are* there, they *do* exist. Depending on the type of adoption arrangement you have, you may see your child or be involved with him or her. But the loss and grief remain. Ours is a very strange dilemma, unlike many others. For those who have chosen to terminate their pregnancy, there may also be a feeling of loss or grief. But that can be real for them, as their child is no more. My child is alive and well, and yet I grieve.

Have you noticed the "waves" in which grief can come and swallow us up? I have gone for long periods of time where I am fine and secure in the decision I made. Then out of the blue I am hit with a wave of grief that crashes over me and swallows me up. Have you experienced that?

Take a minute to reflect on where you are right now. Ask God to be your steadying force and your guide through the highs and lows of your grief. Thank him for being there for you. Ask him to provide people to support you.

FEAR

The fear of the LORD is the beginning of knowledge, but fools despise wisdom and discipline.

—Proverbs 1:7 NIV

WHAT A STRANGE verse. I have always thought of fear as a bad thing. I was afraid of the boogeyman when I was small. I was afraid of failing as I grew up. And now I try and hide my fears so that others don't know what I'm afraid of.

The Bible talks about fear in relation to God a lot. In this verse, we are told that we cannot begin to attain knowledge without first fearing God. Are we supposed to shudder at the thought of him? No. This fear is a loving reverence that includes submission to his lordship and to the commands of his Word.

On the other hand, fools despise wisdom and discipline. A fool is someone who hates knowledge and correction of any kind. A fool says in his heart that God does not exist. Fools rant and rave whenever they feel like it. They rely on themselves to have all the answers for any problem they come up against.

So, before we can move forward in this walk with God, we have to acknowledge that he is God. We must have a healthy fear of him. To put it another way, we have to respect who he is and what he has done, what he can do, and what he will do. We cannot put God in a box and limit him to only caring about our spiritual needs but not our emotional or physical ones.

Which are you today? Are you wise and practice regular fear of God? Or are you a fool and think you have all the answers? Take a minute to write in your journal about who you really are. This journal is just between you and God. He already knows and sees the real you. Maybe you just need to admit it to yourself. Ask him to help you change and grow in your relationship with him.

ABOVE DIAMONDS

A good woman is hard to find, and worth far more than diamonds.
—Proverbs 31:10 NIV

THE WOMAN DESCRIBED in detail in Proverbs 31 is a model for us all. But I don't think any person could embody *everything* listed in that chapter of the Bible. I think it is rather a compilation of the best traits, kind of like a best-case scenario. Just like Jesus is a model for all of humanity, this woman is an example for us specifically; someone who understands what it means to be a woman and a wife and a mother.

The tenth verse sums up the chapter without going into all of the detail. A good woman *is* hard to find. We're out there, but so many of us have been beaten down and defeated and told we're not good enough, strong enough, or pretty enough that we are just over it. We don't care anymore about whatever role it is we are supposed to be playing.

In this chapter, this very godly woman is described as a hard-worker, a seamstress, an early-riser, a savvy business woman, someone who cares about the less-fortunate, wise and a good household manager. Her children and her husband are nuts about her. And why wouldn't they be? She sounds perfect, almost too good to be true.

It's easy to read this and think, *Well, I'm a good business woman. I can sew.* But the deeper truth to this passage is not all of the things this woman *does.* Yes, she is a doer and keeps herself busy. But I truly think the point of the passage is who she is on the inside. We are not children of God and given strength and wisdom and discernment and knowledge because of the things we do. God gives us those things according to who we are. Do we love him? Do we seek to serve him with all that we are? Are we willing to go wherever he calls us and do whatever he asks us to do?

Take a minute and reflect if you are a doer or a be-er. Are you content with who you are? Or are you so busy doing, doing, doing that you can't answer that question? Have you established a growing relationship with God? Ask him to help you be more like him today.

GOSSIP

The words of a gossip are like choice morsels; they go down to a man's inmost parts.

—Proverbs 18:8 NIV

KNOWING EACH OTHER'S business used to be the way of the world. When we all lived in small towns with many generations of the same family, it was hard to get away from it. I grew up in the same small town as my father had. My grandmother and uncle and his family lived there too. Everyone knew who we were. Both my dad and my uncle owned businesses there, so not only did everyone know us, many of them had business dealings with us. You can imagine what it did to the gossip mill when a member of that family—me—got pregnant in high school. Now they all had something to talk about!

The Bible has a lot to say about gossip, gossiping and gossips. The book of Proverbs alone gives us pictures of what this type of person is and how her actions affect those around her. A gossip betrays confidences and separates close friends. Without gossip, a quarrel dies down. In the book of Romans, Paul equates gossips with those who have become filled with every kind of wickedness, evil, greed, and depravity. He says gossips are the same as those full of envy, murder, strife, deceit, and malice. We learn from Timothy that gossiping can be a result of idleness. He goes on to say that busybodies go from house to house saying things they ought not to.

It's hard not to gossip. Let's face it, as women and as people, sometimes we're just curious about what's going on with those around us. Sometimes it's not possible to ask them directly. Sometimes it would be embarrassing to them or to us to ask what is going on. Instead, we ask someone *else* whom we think might know. We ask someone who lives next door to them. Or we ask their close friend. In doing so, we put that other person in an awkward position. It's not fair to ask them those questions. It's not right to think that other people's business is any concern of ours. I think as church goers, it's easy to fall into the trap of "sharing" concerns or prayer requests when it's really gossip. We know an interesting fact or some surprising news about a leader or someone who we all think should be perfect, and we can't wait to tell whoever is available.

Are you able to keep control of your tongue? Are you able to keep things to yourself? What if someone comes to you in total confidence and asks you to please not tell anyone. Maybe what they are sharing with you is not earth-shattering, but maybe they just don't want anyone else to know. Can you be trusted? Are you a gossip? Take a minute right now and ask God to help you honor him in everything you say.

THE PIG

Like a gold ring in a pig's snout is a beautiful face on an empty head.

—Proverbs 11:22

HAVE YOU EVER experienced this? You see someone who is physically attractive, and then they open their mouth. I think the best example of this is our culture's pop stars. I could name names, but why? You know who they are. They are beautiful and popular and have every material possession known to man. But they can't keep a husband, can't keep friends, and live reckless lives without discipline or boundaries. Sometimes they forget to finish getting dressed before leaving the house. They open their mouths to speak, and all that comes out is self-absorbed talk about how they are such a role model and example and how everyone wants to be like them.

Let me ask you something. Do you *really* want to be like that? Do you want people to think you have it all together only to find out you don't? This verse says what a waste it is to give a woman beautiful gifts only to find out she's not what she looks like. What a waste to give someone an attractive body so she can squander it on the pages of a trashy magazine. Even though God knows what decisions we are going to make before we make them, it grieves him when we take the gifts he gives us and throw them away.

What's the point of putting a gold ring in a pig's snout? Is it going to make the pig stop rolling around in the mud? Will it make the pig clean up his living environment? Will it instantly make the pig a moral, upright…well…pig? *No!* Our outward appearance isn't who we are. We can look smart with the right clothes and right hair and right glasses, but the proof is in the pudding. It comes through when we open our mouths and speak and by the way we live our lives. For some, looks define the person because that's all they care about. Their priority is looking this way or owning "this" or having the newest or best "that." But you won't know that for sure without getting to know them.

What are you today? Are you all about looks? Or is there something more to you? Take a minute and reflect on this.

THE LIST

These six things the Lord hates, indeed, seven are an abomination to Him: A proud look [the spirit that makes one overestimate himself and underestimate others], a lying tongue, and hands that shed innocent blood, a heart that manufactures wicked thoughts and plans, feet that are swift in running to evil, a false witness who breathes out lies [even under oath], and he who sows discord among his brethren.

—Proverbs 6:16-19 AMP

HANDS THAT SHED innocent blood...are we not talking about murderers? Is this not the description of someone who takes a life? If a living person has a heart that is beating and something is done to make that heart stop beating, is that not the taking of a life?

Abortion is a hot-button issue in our culture. Everyone has an opinion. It seems like the loudest side is the one with the most money. Advertising, literature, billboards that scream "pro-choice" as if the other side is anti-choice. The implication is that pro-lifers are out to benefit in some crazy way if a woman chooses to carry her baby to term. The funny thing is that *abortion clinics are the only ones making money.* Agencies that offer life-affirming choices offer their services free of charge, are staffed by volunteers and rely on people in the community to financially support them so they can keep their doors open.

So again I ask: aren't hands that shed innocent blood indeed murderers? If a heart is beating before a procedure that is not beating after the procedure is done, is that not murder? Is there anything more innocent than a baby in the womb? A tiny human who has never breathed, never had the opportunity to make a mistake. Is he really to blame?

This is not pro-life rhetoric you're reading. This is God's Word. He says he hates those who shed innocent blood. He says he hates liars. In this passage, he even says he hates those who manufacture wicked thoughts and plans. Have you ever thought up a plan for revenge against a neighbor? A co-worker? A friend? I have. That makes me guilty of this. God makes it clear that he hates this group of people. If I was not a born-again Christian, God would hate me.

Where are you in this? Do you see yourself on that list? God's Word is a mirror in which we can see who and what we really are. Ask God to reveal your true heart to you. Repent of your sins and ask God to forgive you and make you a new creature. Ask him to replace your old ways with his ways.

LIFE AND DEATH

A life devoted to things is a dead life, a stump; a God-shaped life is a flourishing tree.

—Proverbs 11:28

WE LIVE IN a very "thing"-oriented society. Our parents and grandparents couldn't even imagine a world with so many technological advances. We have so many opportunities, so much more flexibility than they ever knew or experienced. As I write this I'm sitting in a coffee shop, writing on a computer with no wires. Weird, eh? It seems like no matter how much we have, it's never enough. Even when we get what we thought we wanted, it fails to satisfy us. We still want more.

My grandmother would turn over in her grave if she knew we had two television sets, two laptops plus a home computer, and three cars. Some of you are surprised that I have so little! What is it about us that drives us to get and get and buy and buy with no hope of ever getting enough?

When Jesus was walking this earth, people had nothing. They walked everywhere they wanted to go. Some trips were hundreds of miles long. They caught or picked and cooked their own food. They lodged at people's houses along the way. They didn't have a lot in terms of things, but they had close, sweet, intimate fellowship with each other. Think about how well you could get to know someone if you walked with them one hundred miles with no radio, no ipod, no cell phone, no computer, no separate rooms at the hotel, or no TV shows to interrupt your discussion.

I often wonder about the wisdom of this age. I know we have lots of technology and lots of things, but look at the fallout from all of these wonderful discoveries: Marriages are failing, our churches have been turned into businesses, and our relationships have been reduced to emails. Are we really better off?

Look at how far we have fallen away from God. I know the Israelites, God's chosen people, struggled with their relationship with God. It's challenging to love and worship and live for a God I have never seen in physical form. Now add to that the noise of emails, cell phones, televisions, and radios and try to maintain a close, sweet, intimate walk with God. No wonder our focus is skewed. No wonder we don't have any power. We are too distracted to focus on God's voice and leading and direction. God will not scream to be heard over all the noise. Rather, his is a still, small voice, and we have to give ourselves time and space in which to hear it.

Where are you in all of this? Have you allowed the white noise of this age to interfere with your relationship with God? Ask him to reveal himself to you in a real way today.

A HEART AT PEACE

A heart at peace gives life to the body, but envy rots the bones.
—Proverbs 14:30 NIV

WHAT'S THE SECRET to long life? Is it a fountain of youth? Is it diet and exercise? Or is it a heart at peace? What a concept. Living a life of peace with yourself and your family and your Maker.

I am often fascinated to hear older people talk about how they continue to maintain a fast pace and an active lifestyle. They talk about doing everything with their spouse including laundry, housework, yard work, shopping and…you name it. You can see in their faces that they truly enjoy being together.

Cancer patients are often told that one of the secrets to their continued health and survival is not medical at all. Rather, it is the support and love and care of family and friends. Doctors regularly encourage family members to join the patient during chemotherapy to talk, read, or play games. They encourage on-going family contact to help raise the patient's mood and well-being. And while it's not medical, it is amazing how those patients compare to ones who live alone and are estranged from their families and don't have close friends.

Sin is the same way. Sin will eat away at our health and well-being. It's hard to believe, I know, especially when those people who are not living according to God's Word look healthy and successful and happy. But there we go again, basing our judgments on looks. God sees the heart, and only he knows what a person's true motives and attitudes are. We can get a pretty good idea by looking at the fruit of a person's life. The fruit is what defines them. The thing we have to remember is that the fruit does not make the person godly; it's the other way around. Out of a relationship with God and a heart that truly wants to do right come good, healthy fruit.

Which of these define you? Is your heart at peace? Or are you running faster and faster, trying to keep up with the world around you? Or trying to live up to someone else's expectations of you? The only model we need to look at is the one Jesus gives us in the Bible. Now, I know what you're thinking! That's a lot to live up to, right? It's not that we need to live up to it. We are not able to do that because we are human, and God is…well…God.

But the Bible is our road map. Our standard. Our guide to this life. In it we find no pressure to live up to the standard our neighbor is setting. We find no pressure to work the most hours or be the most successful. Rather, we will find encouragement for everyday living. God loves us and created us each to be different—on purpose. We're not supposed to be just like our seemingly perfect neighbor. We're not supposed to live up to what other people think we should be, do, or look like. God is the only one who matters. He is more concerned about the content of our character than how we dress, how we fix our hair, and how much money we make.

Are you at peace? Are you able to lay your head down at night and rest, knowing you are right with God? Or are you kept awake by the pressures of this life? Ask God to reveal himself to you in a personal way. Ask him to show you his standard for your life. Ask him to help you block out all the other voices that are calling to you and setting a standard for you that God never intended.

THE BODY

God wants the combination of his steady, constant calling and warm, personal counsel in Scripture to come to characterize us, keeping us alert for whatever he will do next. May our dependably steady and warmly personal God develop maturity in you so that you get along with each other as well as Jesus gets along with us all. Then we'll be a choir—not our voices only, but our very lives singing in harmony in a stunning anthem to the God and Father of our Master Jesus!
—Romans 15:3-6

O UR MUSIC MINISTER recently told us that a choir resembles a small body of Christ. The parallels are obvious; each section of the choir sings a different part, and each person within each section has differing strengths and weaknesses compared to the people on their right and left. He told us that as choir members we are church leaders and because of that fact we needed to keep ourselves pure as we seek to serve God and lead our church.

Then it hit me. I think I finally "got" it. As a body of believers we are supposed to care about each other in such a way that it is *not* okay with us if our brother is living in sin. It is *not* okay with us for our sister to come to church on Sunday and live how she wants to the rest of the week.

What a revelation! This passage of Scripture tells us what God is doing. Our ultimate goal here on this earth is to become more and more like Jesus. As brothers and sisters in Christ, we are to allow God to use us in the lives of others as well as allow others to sow into our lives. An eye by itself does not know how to walk and talk. But combined with the rest of the body, the eye is a very important part that keeps us on the road and keeps us from running into things.

It's the same way in a church. No one member can know all and be all. But if we are all united in the same effort, if we are all using our different gifts and talents for the good of everybody, then we can all grow and mature and become more like Jesus.

Are you living a pure life? Are you allowing wise counsel in your life and learning from others? Are you allowing God to work through you to help others? Ask God to show you opportunities to serve him and learn more about him.

EZEKIEL

…preach against the prophets of Israel who are making things up out of their own heads and calling it "prophesying." Preach to them the real thing. Tell them, "Listen to God's Message!" God, the Master, pronounces doom on the empty-headed prophets who do their own thing and know nothing of what's going on!

—Ezekiel 13:1-3

I KNOW WHAT you're thinking; this is Old Testament and doesn't apply to us, right? I've thought the same thing myself. But I think the people who worked and lived and wrote in this era went through a lot, and if they didn't learn a lot, then their sufferings could at least benefit those of us who are reading about them centuries later.

Ezekiel was given a very unpleasant assignment. He was the mouthpiece that went against what everyone was saying in his day. If you would have watched the evening news, you would have believed that everyone was hearing from God, everyone was prophesying in the name of God and that everyone was on the same page. This simply was not true.

Let's use our imagination and try to put ourselves in Ezekiel's shoes for a moment. Everything on the evening news is either a partial truth, a distortion of the truth, or an outright lie. Oprah isn't the do-gooder everyone thinks she is; in fact, she's an antichrist and a forerunner to the end of the world. Technology, while not inherently good or bad, seeks to separate and fill minds with filth and themes that are distinctly anti-Christian. The morality of the world is going down the toilet. "Good" is called "bad" while "bad" is called "good." At the same time all this is happening, society seems to be experiencing a huge spiritual awakening, in which everyone is involved in some type of spirituality. Spiritual leaders whom we used to be able to trust are now trying to turn traditional Christianity on its head. Ezekiel alone is called to be salt and light in a world that is going crazy.

Now, when put in that context, is Ezekiel really that far removed from us? Even though his ministry took place some 500 years before Christ, do you find any similarities between his challenges and yours? I do. His call isn't so different from ours. As Christians, we are called to be light in a world that is dark and getting darker. We are called to be a preservative to our culture, fighting the "new age" in favor of the Christ-centered, Bible-based truth.

Are you salty? Are you seeking to preserve truth? Or are you contributing to its demise? Ask God to empower you, to fill you with his Spirit and his wisdom as you seek to be light in a dying world.

THE REAL THING

I can't believe your fickleness—how easily you have turned traitor to him who called you by the grace of Christ by embracing a variant message! It is not a minor variation, you know; it is completely other, an alien message, a no-message, a lie about God.

—Galatians 1:6-7

I WORKED ONE summer at a theme park that had a heavy influx of international tourists. The risk of receiving counterfeit money was very real. Several times the restaurant had been stuck with a fake fifty or one-hundred-dollar bill. Over time, that added up to real goods exchanged for money with no value. As workers, we were schooled on how to spot the fake. We were given pens that would turn the paper money a different color if it was phony. Since the point of the theme park was making money, spotting a counterfeit bill was of high importance.

So how did we know what was real and what was fake? How did we learn to spot the differences? What was the standard they used to teach us the distinction? In order to know how to spot phony money, we studied the real thing. We got used to the feel of the paper, the raised quality of the ink, the look of the watermarks and their position on the currency. We learned which famous person appeared on what bill. We spent dedicated, intentional time getting to know the real thing so when a phony bill came around, we could recognize it.

Can you recognize a counterfeit dollar bill? How about a counterfeit Christian? How about people who say they believe in God but then live their lives contrary to that? *What if the person is preaching?* This is so applicable to us. How many of us have been sucked into a church by the glitz and glamour, the laid-back atmosphere and the simple messages, only to get down the road and realize there is no substance? It's scary that so many people are getting fooled into something that claims to be Christian but really isn't.

How do we recognize what is from God and what isn't? Our best bet is to study the real thing. Our "real thing" is the Bible—God's Word. It is the inspired Word of God given to men. It has not changed in two thousand years. Its message does not change with the times. It is as culturally relevant today as it was then.

The only way we are going to identify a real Christian from a phony one is to know the Creator. He formed us and made us. Christianity is his idea. Going to heaven and living eternally is his idea. If we get to know him and the heart he has for his people, we will be able to spot a fake a mile away.

I challenge you to get to know the God of the Bible. Don't know how to start? Pick up your Bible and start reading the book of John. There is no denying his power. Once you know him, no one else will compare.

SLAVERY

Do you think I speak this strongly in order to manipulate crowds?
Or curry favor with God? Or get popular applause? If my goal was
popularity, I wouldn't bother being Christ's slave.

—Galatians 1:10-12

OH, THE UNPREDICTABILITY of popularity! One minute
you're in, the next minute you're out. One day your clothes are
in fashion, the next day they're not. One month you're wearing the
right color, the next month you're out. It's hard to keep up. Look at the
presidential polls. One day we like him and think he's doing a good job;
the next month we want to impeach him. What is it with our society?
Who seems to be driving the vote of popular opinion? Have you ever
found yourself bucking the system and doing your own thing?

Paul wrote this as a letter from a pastor who loves his people. His
goal was to remind the church of the freedom we have in Christ. Being
a Christian isn't a list of rules and regulations. Rather, it is the freedom
to know God and surrender ourselves and our lives to him to use as he
pleases.

Being a Christian oftentimes feels like swimming upstream. We're
not usually popular in our views and our beliefs. We're not popular
when we become vocal about the offensive nature of pop music and
network television shows. People label us as zealous and radical and try
to silence our views. But why should we be surprised? This is exactly

what the religious leaders of the day did to Paul. Tradition tells us that he was beheaded on a public road so word would spread quickly that he was finally dead. Why should we expect any less?

In this age of tolerance it seems that anyone can say anything they want no matter how wrong or offensive. And we have to put up with it because of free speech, except when it comes to Christians. Anyone can say anything they want to about us, but we're not allowed to respond. We're not allowed to do anything but take it. If we do speak out about it, we are further slandered.

As Christians our sole focus on this earth is to please God. This is hardly ever a popular thing. We need to decide if we are going to please God or please man, and then we need to do it. If we are going to please man, we need to be willing to take the good with the bad and to cycle between popular and unpopular. If we are going to please God, we need to focus on him alone and shut out all the other voices.

What's it going to be for you today? Take a minute and reflect on this in your journal. Ask God to show you what is right and to give you the strength to do it.

LOVE

But the fruit of the Spirit is love…

—Galatians 5:22 NIV

H AVE YOU EVER thought of yourself as a tree? As women, we
are created to be life-givers. We bear "fruit" in the obvious sense:
children are born out of our bodies much like an apple tree bears apples.
But God created us to bear something more than children. As we grow
in him and in our relationship with him, our spiritual roots go deep.
We begin to see changes in our lives that may not be conscious.

One of those changes is love. We naturally love those close to us,
but did you know that there are different kinds of love? Phileo love
refers to a type of brotherly love that we have for one another. It is not
an all-encompassing love, but rather a friendly type of love that we have
for our friends and others in our realm of influence.

God, on the other hand, has a very special kind of love for us.
Agape love is an all-encompassing, all-surpassing kind of love. It's hard
to articulate exactly the lengths this type of love would go to ensure
we live with him forever in heaven. Did you know that Jesus died on
the cross for *you*? Have you ever personalized the crucifixion like that?
He didn't die some random, tortuous death so that nice, church-going
people could go to heaven. He went to the cross knowing *your* name
and *your* sins and *your* past, present, and future. He died before you or
your parents or grandparents or great-grandparents were even conceived.

Agape love is the model for us. As Christians, we are sinful and fallen, with pasts full of poor choices. The good news for us is that when we turn to faith in Christ, that slate is wiped clean. However, for many of us, we have learned wrong patterns of loving. For many of us, it is hard to change habits that we have lived with for so long. We try to love our neighbor and do what the Bible says, but we are not able to do that on our own. We don't have the ability to love our neighbor as ourselves. But God has that ability. He has the capacity to love us in a way no human can ever understand.

That's where the roots I was talking about come in. As growing Christians, we are deepening and strengthening those roots every day as we read the Bible, spend time in prayer, go to church, or go to a Bible study. Those roots tap into God's love, and suddenly we find ourselves loving the unlovable not because we want to or suddenly find something about them that's lovable, but because we are growing in Christ and the number one fruit of being a true Christian is love. Love for God, love for ourselves, and love for our fellow man is a natural result of pursuing God and getting to know him and asking him to fill us, change us, and make us more like him.

Take a minute to reflect on God's love for you. Since becoming a Christian, do you see a change in how you love yourself and others? If you are not yet a Christian, why not take that step right now? Ask God to come into your heart and life and make you a new creature in him.

JOY

But the fruit of the Spirit is…joy…

—Galatians 5:22 NIV

MY SISTER-IN-LAW'S NAME is Joy. I love the attitude her name reflects, and her name truly fits. Joy has a zest for life and a love for her family that I haven't seen often. The Bible says that the joy of the Lord is our strength. Isn't that interesting? Our strength is not found in God's might or power or lordship over everything, but in the joy we have in our lives just knowing him.

This joy isn't happiness based on the successes in our lives. We aren't joyful *because* we got a promotion at work or found the right boyfriend or bought an outfit that we love. Rather, this is a joy that springs out of us as a result of knowing God. This is one of those examples of "being" versus "doing." True joy can't come as a result of anything we do. True joy springs out of us as a result of knowing and loving Jesus.

Do you have joy in your life? Sometimes it can be hard to define what joy is. Happiness counts. Contentment is part of it. But it's more than that. It's being okay no matter what comes at you in life. It's actually being more than okay. It's the ability to be triumphant and to exclaim with no reservation that God is fully in control. It's being as sure of God's control of your life as you are on your best day. Sounds like a tall order, doesn't it?

It's the picture of the fruit tree all over again. We can't expect to accept Christ as our Lord and Savior and continue in our old life style. If we planted a tree and wanted to produce healthy, ripe, shiny, edible fruit, we wouldn't water only occasionally, cover the tree so it doesn't get any sun, and feed it poison, would we?

That's the same with us. We can't continue in our old lifestyle and hope to bear healthy fruit. That fruit is evidence of God's work in our lives. But if we don't make a way for him to work, he can't work in us and through us and produce things like joy.

Think of it this way. What if you wanted to grow your own apples? What would you do? Well, you would go to Home Depot, get a peach tree and plant it in your yard, right? Maybe not. But that's kind of the point. If you want to produce the fruit of the spirit of God, you have to follow the directions. You can't sow seeds of lying and cheating and stealing and expect to produce joy and peace and patience that just oozes out of you in times of turmoil. These things have to be cultivated.

Do you have joy in your life that wells up from your heart and spills out on to everyone around you? Take a minute and think about where you are and where you want to be. Ask God to help you learn how to cultivate joy in your heart.

PEACE

But the fruit of the Spirit is…peace…

—Galatians 5:22 NIV

I'VE GOT PEACE like a river, I've got peace like a river, I've got peace like a river in my soul…" Have you ever been on or near a body of water early in the morning when the surface looks less like water and more like glass? It's amazing to me that those molecules of water would be resting enough all at the same time to make it look so smooth and calm. Even the ocean is usually calmer in the morning before the winds pick up and stir the waves.

Peace is kind of like this. Actually, I think there is more than one kind of peace. One type of peace is the kind that seems to take over in times of crisis, the times when you are going along in your life and suddenly the bottom drops out. Good examples are a death in the family, an unexpected pregnancy, or the sudden end to a close relationship. It's scary how those times can happen when we least expect them.

When we look back, it's sometimes easy to see how God was preparing us for that time, or all things seemed to point to it happening, but we couldn't—or wouldn't—see it. While I don't advocate denial as a lifestyle, I do believe God sometimes protects us from seeing what's coming. If we knew what was coming, we would have more time to be anxious, more time to make our own plans, and we would be less dependent on God to get us through those situations. Instead, God doesn't always allow us to see or understand what's coming. He uses that opportunity to pour out his peace on us when it seems least likely.

A second kind of peace is that deep-down stillness in our souls. Even without a crisis, most of our lives are a whirlwind of activity. With work, school, church, exercise, or other activities, most of us are busy from dawn until dusk. We also have the worries of this life like paying bills, saving for the future, and paying for our purchases. Even with these stresses, though, God provides us with a bottomless sense of peace that radiates from deep within our souls.

The discipline is in the balance. The balance comes from having the right priorities in the right order, which is so much easier said than done. Now, will having the right priorities in the right order instantly produce peace? No, this peace I'm talking about goes far deeper. But the Holy Spirit lives in each believer. The voice of the Holy Spirit is still and quiet and we therefore have to work at hearing it. I believe the first step in this is taking the unnecessary clutter and noise out of our lives. We can achieve that by looking over our priorities, putting them in the correct order, and forgetting the rest.

Do you have peace like a river today? What are you willing to do to get that peace? Ask God to help you by showing you his priorities. Ask him for the strength to live those priorities out.

PATIENCE

But the fruit of the Spirit is…patience…

—Galatians 5:22 NIV

I LEARNED A song when I was a little girl. I think I learned it in Lavaliers, which was a church-based version of Girl Scouts. The song went something like this: "Have patience, don't be in such a hurry; when you get impatient, you only start to worry; remember that God has patience too and think of all the times when others have to wait on you." That about sums it up, doesn't it? Don't we most often associate patience with waiting on something or someone? I once had someone tell me not to pray for patience unless I wanted to be seriously tested.

So, how patient are you? The way God builds our faith and deepens our walk with him is to give us opportunities to trust him. For example, if we pray for patience, he's going to give us lots of opportunities to practice that exact thing. If you pray for patience, you can expect to hit every red light, a line at the check-out counter, and computers that don't work like they are supposed to. God is funny that way. He doesn't just give us something like patience overnight, and one morning we wake up and have it. Rather, he builds these things into us by challenging us to rely on him more and more.

If you want to be a more patient person, and I mean *really want to be more patient*, ask God to help you. Then look for opportunities to trust him. Experience has taught me that those situations will show up all

175

around you once you start asking. You may have to really pay attention to see some of them, but take this as a sign that God has heard your prayer and wants to help you.

Another kind of patience is waiting on something unseen. Maybe you have been praying for something for a long time. Perhaps you have been praying that God would deliver you from a job you don't like or a bad living situation or depression. Maybe you have become a Christian and have started praying for your friends and family members. While you wait, God is building your character and deepening your faith in him. As you pray, you are getting the added benefit of learning patience that you can transfer to other areas of your life.

How is your patience quota? How are you at waiting on God to hear you and answer your prayers? Are you ready for God to work in your heart and make you a more patient person? Take a minute right now to ask him to help you.

KINDNESS

But the fruit of the Spirit is…kindness…

—Galatians 5:22 NIV

WHAT DO YOU think of when you hear the word "kindness"? Does that word make you think of the word "nice"? What about "good"? Kindness is a fruit of the spirit like love, joy, and patience. When we begin walking with God and going deeper with him, we will begin to exhibit kindness in our character. But what is kindness and what does it look like?

At its simplest, kindness is being nice to other people and to animals. It's being nice to our neighbors, people we see in the grocery store, and those we work with. These are not necessarily people we would pick to be our friends. Rather, these are people whom God has placed in our path to challenge us and help us grow in our walk with him. While being kind to other people will not make us closer to God, it will facilitate the growth process as we seek to be more like him.

To understand kindness better, think about your relationship with God. You know the type of person you are; you know your history, your mistakes, and your bad choices. Yet God chooses to show kindness to you whether you worship him or not. He chose to die on the cross for you, knowing all the mistakes you have made and will make in the future. It is because of God's kindness to us that we even desire his forgiveness and his love in our lives. It is truly God's kindness that leads us to repentance.

Consider some of the synonyms for "nice": polite, good, pleasant, and careful. Note the synonyms for "kind": compassion, gentleness, thoughtfulness, consideration. See any differences? The word kind is a deeper commentary on the type of person you're dealing with. This is a person who is more than skin-deep. Many of us can appear nice on the outside. It's sometimes actually easier to be nice to strangers in the grocery store than it is to treat our own family right. Have you noticed that about yourself?

True kindness is delivered to all persons equally, regardless of who they are. This is much easier said than done. Why is it so easy to treat a stranger better than our own family? Not an easy answer. This is where the power of God at work in our lives comes in to play. It seems as though we need an extra dose of *something* in order to treat right those closest to us. Why is that? Is it because we know they love us? Because we know they won't leave, that they can't leave?

Are you a kind person? Are you kind to those within your family as well as those strangers in the grocery store? Ask God to develop kindness in you. Ask him to show you opportunities to show kindness to others. Thank him for his kindness to you in spite of yourself.

GOODNESS

But the fruit of the Spirit is…goodness…

—Galatians 5:22 NIV

THIS IS NOT a word we hear often anymore when describing people. True goodness is hard to find in our world. Doing good for others just because we want to, not because we want something in return, is harder and harder to find. But I have found that one way to help myself out of depression, a poor attitude, or a tough day is to treat others kindly, love them through my actions, do something nice for them without expecting anything in return. Sometimes when I feel the most rushed I make sure to hold the door open for someone or let them go ahead of me in line. I know how crazy that sounds. But putting others in front of me often helps my bad mood start to change.

What does goodness look like in *your* life? How do you treat others with decency and integrity? How do you treat *yourself* with decency and integrity? As women and as people, we have to take care of ourselves before we can take care of anyone else. I know that is a great idea, but sometimes putting it into practice can be challenging. We are born caretakers. If someone stays home with the children, it's usually Mom. We are natural nurturers. That is who God made us to be. But in all that nurturing of others, let's not lose ourselves. We have to work hard to carve out our own little piece of peace and serenity.

What brings you rest and relaxation? For some it's reading or exercising or journaling. For others it's taking long walks. Find something that refreshes you and restores your soul. We can't give away something we don't possess ourselves. Therefore it's hard to give away goodness if we are worn down, tired, and empty. It's important to work soul-restoring activities into your life in order to live the life God intended for you. I know that taking time out just for you can feel selfish, but don't let that stop you. Jesus took time to pray in private, walk, and work alone. He created us to need each other but to still spend time away being refreshed.

So, where are you today? Are you full and can easily show goodness to those around you, to friends and strangers alike? Or do you feel empty, like you have nothing to give to anyone? Ask God to fill you and restore you. Then ask him to show you opportunities to show goodness to others.

FAITHFULNESS

But the fruit of the Spirit is…faithfulness…

—Galatians 5:22 NIV

WHAT DOES BEING faithful mean to you? Why is a faithful God important to us? Why do we value faithfulness in marriage? In work? Why is this considered a fruit of the spirit? How come as we grow in our relationship with God, we become more and more faithful? And why does it matter?

All good questions. Faithfulness is an important key to our relationship with God and with others. So, what is it? "Faithfulness" is *the quality of keeping commitments in relationships*. This is such a simple definition for such an important word. Faithfulness is a character trait that is produced when we set our hearts on God and on following him and living for him. Faithfulness follows as we desire and work toward being faithful.

We don't become faithful merely by being good and following all of the "rules" God gives us. The truth is that we are not able to follow the rules and be good on our own. We are not able because we are fallen and sinful. Only Jesus Christ was able to live a perfect, sinless life. We are able to navigate our way through this life only if Jesus lives in our hearts and helps us. Only by that happening will we see faithfulness become part of who we are.

So, why does keeping our commitments matter? If we call ourselves Christians, it matters. If we tell others that God is the most important thing to us, it matters. Being a Christian means we are called to be set apart, to be different than the world. Do you see many people keeping their commitments these days? How many divorced people do you know? How many people are living on credit? How many people in your church promise to tithe, but then decide to use the money another way? How about people who commit to serving in the church or community but are too busy to go to the meetings? What about those "do-gooders" who are involved in everything but are such poor time managers nothing gets done? Are you one of those people? Am I talking to you?

This is not what God has called us to do. This is not who God has called us to be. He has called us to be faithful to our word, firm in our commitments so that if we say we are going to do something, we do. If we commit to something with our mouth, we should let nothing stand in our way of honoring that promise. We should *not* be quick to commit to things, but instead pray about them and ask God if this is something he has for us. It's okay to say no. *It's okay to say no!* The Bible urges us to let our "yes" be a commitment and let our "no" be firm.

So, where are you today? Are you a faithful person? Do you over commit? Do you let your schedule rule you instead of the other way around? Take a minute and ask God to show you how to be more faithful. Ask him to grow the fruit of faithfulness in you from the inside out.

GENTLENESS

But the fruit of the Spirit is…gentleness…

—Galatians 5:23 NIV

WHAT DOES GENTLENESS mean to you? This is another one of those words that we don't seem to hear or use much anymore. Someone who is kind and gentle seems…well…outdated. Some references to gentleness include "gentle giant" or a "gentle rain." A close synonym to gentle is "meek." Meekness implies a submissive spirit, and may even indicate undue submission in the face of insult or injustice. To me, gentleness sounds like someone who is a wimp, someone who lets others walk all over them.

Jesus was the embodiment of gentleness. There were a lot of people who didn't like him, who tried to catch him in lies, who tried to trick him into doing something wrong. He had plenty of reasons to attack those people and tell them what they were doing wrong. He could have revealed himself for who he really was—the God of the universe—and inflicted some plague or some disease on them. He could have had them struck down by lightning. One word to his angels and they could have reduced the victim to a pile of ashes. We see these things actually happen in other areas of the Bible. There are verses where Jesus routed out wrongdoers and delivered justice on the spot.

But there are so many places where Jesus could do that and doesn't. Instead of doling out justice, he is calm and gentle in the face of accusations and lies. Instead of fighting back, he is so secure in his relationship with his heavenly Father that he knows when the timing is right, God will avenge and God will repay.

Do you think Jesus was a wimp? Do you think he let people walk all over him? Or do you think he was modeling for us how we could act—maybe how we are *supposed* to act—in the face of any circumstance? Gentleness is the opposite of "selfish ambition." Gentle people are not "conceited, provoking and envying each other." Gentleness is an expression of humility, considering the needs and hurts of others before one's personal goals.

Where do you fall on this scale? Do you put others ahead of yourself, or do you put your need to be right or your need to repay wrong for wrong, ahead of everything else? Jesus was a model for the ancient people, and he is a model for us now. Take a minute and ask God to grow the fruit of gentleness in your life. Ask him to give you opportunities to show gentleness in unlikely circumstances.

SELF-CONTROL

But the fruit of the Spirit is…self-control.

—Galatians 5:23 NIV

NOW WE COME to the last fruit on the list. I have actually wondered why self-control is last. Is it because it is the least important? How does one get to be the last on a list? Does placement matter, or is it important merely because it is included on the list at all? The list of fruits numbers nine, but I'm sure we could think of others that are not on the list. The fact of the matter is these are character traits, not a check-list for us to follow in order to be some sort of super-Christian.

Self-control. What is it and how do we know if we have it or not? Webster defines "self-control" as *control of one's emotions, desires, or actions by one's own will.* The IVP Bible Commentary defines self-control as the opposite of self-indulgence. Those who are Spirit-led will not indulge the sinful nature. They do not use other people to gratify their own appetites. They have the strength to say no to themselves and to the desires of their sinful nature.

Here's the litmus test: When something tempts you, what do you do? Do you think it's better to be with a guy who is not walking with God than to be alone? Do you stay out too late on Saturday nights so getting up for church Sunday morning is difficult? Are you tempted by porn? Drugs? Alcohol? Each one of us is different. We have different weaknesses. We have diffcrent histories.

But we *do* have a common enemy. Satan prowls around this earth like a hungry lion looking for someone to devour. He has nothing better to do than to watch us and get to know us and our weaknesses. Believe me, if you are attempting in any way to live for God, Satan is watching you and knows what your weaknesses are. He knows what makes you leave the straight and narrow path you are trying so hard to stay on. He is a master of disguise. Don't expect to be confronted head-on with temptation. Rather, expect the unexpected. Expect subtleness. Expect the slippery-slope approach, where the first step isn't that big of a deal. And the second step isn't that big of a deal either. But before long, you seem to be a long way from where you intended to be.

Self-control starts now. It starts every day, asking God to shine his bright light in all of your dark places. We are only as strong as our weakest part. *Every decision makes a difference.* We are living out today the results of yesterday's decisions. It's not always the big decisions that are the most toxic. It is often the small ones along the way that can throw us off course.

Where are you today? Are you on target with where God wants you to be? Ask him to reveal your weaknesses to you. God's strength is made perfect in our weakness. Ask him to fill in your weak places with his strength. Ask him to give you discernment to recognize when you are being tempted. Temptation can be subtle, but God can help you see it when it comes your way.

BELT OF TRUTH

Therefore put on the full armor of God, so that when the day of evil comes, you may be able to stand your ground, and after you have done everything, to stand. Stand firm then, with the belt of truth buckled around your waist...

—Ephesians 6:13-14 NIV

WHEN YOU GET dressed each morning, what is the first thing you put on? What is the second? When you put on your makeup, what is the first thing that goes on? The answer is the foundation. What do these foundations do for us? Well, they hold us together and make us a little more presentable to the rest of the world.

The armor of God is like this. We can be dressed up, made up, prettied up, prepared, and organized. But if we are not "prayed up," then we are exposed, vulnerable to any attacks that come our way.

What am I talking about? If you are a Christian, the armor of God is something you need every second of every hour of every day. The best way to ensure that you are prepared for whatever lies ahead is to get into the habit of putting it on each morning. How do we do that? By first understanding what it is and then prayerfully putting it on a piece at a time.

The first item is the belt of truth. What is the purpose of a belt? It holds up our pants. It's a very practical item. The belt is located around the waist and is the central piece of the armor. The other pieces either surround this one or are connected to it. The truth of God needs to be central to our lives. We need to get the Word of God, the Bible, into our heads and build our lives on its foundation.

Jesus was not a warrior in the way we think of a warrior. He didn't wear physical armor and wield a weapon. But he was a warrior in the spiritual sense. He knew the Bible and was always ready to answer anyone who challenged it or asked a question about it. He won people over with his character and his kindness, not by his brute force.

What kind of warrior are you? Do you know what you believe and why you believe it? Take a minute now to ask God to help you understand him better. If you have not yet done so, ask Jesus to come into your heart and make you a new person.

BREASTPLATE OF RIGHTEOUSNESS

Therefore put on the full armor of God, so that when the day of evil comes, you may be able to stand your ground, and after you have done everything, to stand. Stand firm then… with the breastplate of righteousness in place…

—Ephesians 6:13-14 NIV

THE SECOND PIECE of armor is the breastplate. This is something we don't see much of anymore, but it is vital to soldiers. Today's solider refers to it as body armor, but it's the same thing. The breastplate is a solid piece of armor that goes over the chest. Its main function is to protect the vital organs. This armor can withstand a bullet without giving way. It will make an arrow fall to the ground without sticking. And it will protect the wearer from other bumps and bruises from punches, kicks, or other airborne objects.

The breastplate is also about a person's character. A righteous man is one who is morally upright, without guilt or sin. Jesus was a truly righteous man, the only one who ever lived. We can be made righteous through God, but on our own we don't stand a chance.

If we put all these things together, what do we get? The breastplate of righteousness that keeps us from harm the enemy throws our way, as well as saving us from ourselves. Once again, character is the real issue.

So, what is character? Character is who we are when no one is looking. It's easy to act the right way or say the right thing with other people looking on. But what do you do behind closed doors? Would you do that if others were looking? Do you say one thing in public and another in private?

Do you say you read your Bible regularly? Do you say you have private prayer time with God each day? Do you really do those things? Or are you motivated by what other people think about you. You want them to hold you in high esteem, so you say the things that will help you reach that goal. You see, it really doesn't matter what other people think of you. *Really.* God sees all and knows all. So if you are saying one thing and doing another, the only person who knows is God. And the only person whom it hurts is God. So really, the only person that matters is God. Make sense?

Take a minute to reflect on these things. Take time to ask God to help you be a wholly integrated being who talks and thinks and acts the same whether someone is watching you or not.

GOSPEL OF PEACE

Therefore put on the full armor of God, so that when the day of evil comes, you may be able to stand your ground, and after you have done everything, to stand. Stand firm then...with your feet fitted with the readiness that comes from the gospel of peace...

—Ephesians 6:13-15 NIV

WHAT TYPE OF physical activity do you like to do? Run? Lift weights? Aerobics? I love to Jazzercise, which is a combination of aerobics, kickboxing, and pilates. I love the loud music and the energy I gain from the other class participants. I've been wearing the same clothes to work out in for over six years now. I don't particularly care how I look that early in the morning. What matters to me is that my workout clothes are comfortable and can move with me.

But six years in the same aerobic shoes? I don't think so. I could never make it. I can tell right away when my shoes go out and I need new ones. That happened to me recently and I couldn't figure out what was wrong with me. Usually I jot down the purchase date on the inside of my shoes. That way I can keep track. Then, about 100 hours into the use of those shoes, I can start planning to purchase new shoes. But I had failed to do that and all of a sudden my feet, knees, hips, and back were killing me. I would be fine during the actual class, but the next morning I would get out of bed like a very old lady! Finally a friend asked me if I needed new shoes. How could I have missed that?

Shoes are important! They make or break an outfit. The right shoes can mean success or failure in sports, dancing, hiking, boating, you name it. Shoes are also very important for battle. When soldiers are in battle, they need to ensure good footing at all times. One slip and the enemy can get the upper hand and take them out. Soldiers travel over all types of terrain. It's important their feet stay warm, dry, and healthy so they can maneuver and do what is needed. A soldier's feet need to be ready to move at a moment's notice, which is why they sleep with their boots on.

Having God in your heart will give you the strength and the will to stand your ground and fight the enemy. He will give you steady footing over ground that can be uneven and scary. Take a minute now and thank him for the gift of his peace, which allows you to stand amidst the storms and trials of life.

SHIELD OF FAITH

Therefore put on the full armor of God…In addition to all this, take up the shield of faith, with which you can extinguish all the flaming arrows of the evil one.

—Ephesians 6:13-16 NIV

WEBSTER DEFINES "SHIELD" as *a person or thing that protects.* We see police officers use shields in riot situations or when there is a bomb threat. We see soldiers use shields in movies like *Gladiator* and *Braveheart.* Before the age of lighter weight materials, shields were made of thick pieces of wood. Soldiers would soak them in water overnight. As a result, the wood swelled and the shield would become even heavier.

These heavy, wet shields served a very important purpose. Troops used to shoot flaming arrows at each other. The arrows were swift and could take out a soldier with one hit. The fire would catch on to buildings, grass, or people and wreak havoc. But those who were prepared used their shields for safety. They could block the arrows with it, and the moisture would put out the flames. In times of intense battle, the soldiers formed a line and, crouching behind their shields, would advance forward to meet their attacker.

Does any of this sound like your life? This is what faith is like. If you are a Christian, if you have surrendered your life to Christ, this shield is very important. Your faith is what keeps you standing in the midst of every trial, every tempting situation. It's what keeps you going when the doubts and fears enter your mind. In times of sadness, your faith in Christ comforts you.

The flaming arrows from the enemy are very real. See if you recognize any of these: "You've already screwed your life up so much no one, not even God, can help you." "I can't believe you gave away your baby. What kind of person does that?" "You're not good enough/pretty enough/smart enough." These are lies straight from the pit of hell. These aren't you and don't describe you. If you are a Christian, you have been purchased by the blood of Jesus. He died for you so that you can live. Because you have your shield of faith in place, those arrows don't hit their target, which is your heart.

We all have good days and bad days. Some days are better than others. But faith is not about feeling good. Faith is standing on the fact that God loves you and has a plan for your life. It's about believing that and clinging to it no matter what happens, no matter what situations come your way. Take a minute and thank God for giving you the shield of faith that protects you from all the flaming arrows of the enemy.

HELMET OF SALVATION

Therefore put on the full armor of God, so that when the day of evil comes, you may be able to stand your ground, and after you have done everything, to stand…Take the helmet of salvation …
—Ephesians 6:13,17 NIV

H ELMETS ARE NOT as cool as they used to be. Remember movies with the Roman armies in them, like *Gladiator*? They had really neat helmets: ones with fur or something like that on top; shiny; brassy; sparkly. They could hide your face and protect you from a sword or spear, as well as from anything that may have tried to eat you, like a lion. Today we see helmets for bicycling and riding on a motorcycle. Contact sports use them. But it's just not the same.

In our picture of Christians as soldiers, the helmet is no less important than any other piece of armor. The helmet guards the head from any major wounds that could render us unconscious. Our head is the home of our brain, which houses our mind, our thoughts, our emotions, and our will. The head is a very important part of the body, which is probably why it's called the "head."

The helmet protects our head from harm, but it also serves another function. Our salvation by faith in Jesus Christ is the single most important decision we will ever make. It is God's Word, the Bible, that speaks to us, builds our faith and keeps us going in times of trouble and turmoil. The helmet protects all of that. Satan is called the prince of this world and is out to steal, kill, and destroy us. The best way to do that is to undermine what God has done for us and in us and through us. Look around you. I don't see many magazines, websites, or television shows that encourage us to live boldly and be different from the world. Magazine covers scream conformity in fashion, wrong lifestyle choices, lust for popularity, and greed for more than what God has given us. That helmet of salvation that we put on each and every morning guards us from the enemy's attempts to sabotage God's work in our lives.

I know it's a struggle. I often feel assaulted just by going to the grocery store. It seems like those magazine covers are so blatant they just pierce right through my armor. But I have come to a place where I don't listen to or trust any voice that I don't recognize. I believe that the people who write those magazines do not have my relationship with God as their main concern.

This is a tough topic. Take some time and ask God to help you see him more clearly despite the craziness around you. Take a minute and put on your helmet of salvation—if you haven't already—and ask God to show you his best for you.

THE SWORD OF
THE SPIRIT

Therefore put on the full armor of God, so that when the day of evil
comes, you may be able to stand your ground, and after you have done
everything, to stand…Take the helmet of salvation and the sword of
the Spirit, which is the word of God.

—Ephesians 6:13, 17 NIV

THE FIVE PIECES of armor are the belt, breastplate, shoes, shield,
and helmet. But no suit of armor is complete without a sword.
Notice that the five pieces listed are defensive, which means they serve
as protection. They don't *do* anything. They just sit there, protecting
us from attacks like arrows, swords, punches, or bullets.

But the sword is different. The armor-wearer can maneuver the
sword to strike at something or someone to defend himself from harm.
A sword is a precision instrument; it can be used to stab a specific place.
It can also be used to skin an animal in preparation of eating or making
clothing.

The Bible is our sword. It is a precision instrument that divides bones
and marrow, heart and attitude. When we are in times of trouble or times
of crisis, we can go to the Word of God and find solace, encouragement,
and instruction. How does that happen? Do we flip open the Bible and
read the first verse we see? Not exactly. Our most effective tool in fighting
fears, temptations, and other evils is to know what the Word says. Then
during a time of crisis, we can read what we need to hear.

Let's say everything is going along great. Then, all of a sudden, it's not. You try to have a good attitude, you try to smile, but nothing works. You know something is off. So you open to the book of Ephesians and read in chapter 6 about the full armor of God. The verses tell you to stand, and when you have done that, you stand again. You read about the pieces of armor and you suddenly realize you have not been "putting on" the helmet of salvation. Instead, you have begun believing the lies that you are no good because you chose adoption for your child. You started believing you are unworthy of God's love—or anyone's love for that matter. Your self-esteem went down, and it seemed like things were crashing all around you.

The Bible is a love letter from Jesus. He left it here for us. There will be times when it may be impossible to hear God's voice. But this book is always here for you, whenever you need it. I challenge you today to start reading the Bible regularly. Spend a few minutes each day reading a chapter. Start today in the book of John, and then move on to Romans. Take a minute to reflect on this in your journal. Ask God to help you.

DIVIDE AND CONQUER

Stand united, singular in vision, contending for people's trust in the Message, the good news, not flinching or dodging in the slightest before the opposition. Your courage and unity will show them what they're up against: defeat for them, victory for you—and both because of God. There's far more to this life than trusting in Christ. There's also suffering for him. And the suffering is as much a gift as the trusting...

—Philippians 1:27

ONE OF THE major themes throughout Scripture is the concept of unity or oneness with Christ and also with each other in the body of Christ, the church. Church can be a hard place. Churches, like hospitals, are filled with hurting, sick, dying people. God's plan for the church was for it to be a place of safety, healing, and restoration. But the realities are far from utopian. Heaven will be the culmination of wrapping up life on this earth and receiving new, perfect bodies. Until that day comes, no matter how long we have walked with God, no matter how many years we have known him, we still have the ability to choose sin.

Sin first entered the picture in the Garden of Eden, when Eve chose not the fruit but chose her own will and desires over God's plan. Since then even the most seasoned Christian will be bothered by the temptation to sin from time to time. It's built into our DNA; there's no getting away from it.

Ever since Satan entered the picture he has been at work in the body of Christ which is the church. From a biblical perspective, we are called to live in unity and harmony with one another. But the realities of this world are far from that. Satan knows how strong the church can be. He knows we can be a force for change, a force for good on this planet. He doesn't want that, so he's come up with a two-fold plan to divide and conquer. First, he separates us from God by tempting us with sin. The temptation itself does not do the separating; it's what we do *with* the temptation that matters. Some of us will use a time of temptation to draw nearer to God and depend more heavily on him. Others will choose to give in to the temptation, which leads to sinning against God. At that point we are separated from God and need to make a choice: are we going to remain disconnected from God or are we going to confess our sin and come back into unity with him?

The second part of Satan's attack plan is to separate us from other believers. We were created to be in fellowship with other Christians. How do we know? The Bible tells us that Jesus was in constant fellowship with the twelve, the three, the disciple he loved, and with his father, God. The Trinity is made up of the Father, Son, and Holy Spirit. They are in constant fellowship as one being made up of three distinct parts. We were created in God's image; therefore we were created to be in fellowship. Satan knows this is part of our strength, part of God's design to hold each other up and bear each other's burdens. So he seeks to separate us from each other by isolating us through depression, discouragement, addictions, workaholism, and the like.

So, where are you? Are you standing in unity with the body of Christ? Are you connected to a church? Or are you letting something separate you from God and your church? Ask God to help you see clearly. Ask God to restore your unity with him.

FORGET WHAT IS BEHIND

Forgetting what is behind and straining toward what is ahead, I press on toward the goal to win the prize for which God has called me heavenward in Christ Jesus.

—Philippians 3:13-14 NIV

I LOVE THIS passage because it encourages me to forget what is behind me and look to the future. Although my adoption experience was many years ago, it seems like choices I have made since then still trip me up. It's easy for me to get down on myself for being pregnant and not married in the first place.

The writer of Philippians is telling us to forget about all that; we can't change the past. But what we can do is make good choices from now on.

I plan on going to heaven when I die. I made a decision to follow Jesus Christ as my personal Lord and Savior during my pregnancy. While I would love to say I have been faithful to that commitment every single day, I would be lying.

But that's what is so great about God; we are *never* out of his reach. Never, ever, *ever* have we done something or gone somewhere that he cannot get to us and bring us back.

Won't you trust Him today to change your future?

OBEDIENCE

And being found in appearance as a man, he humbled himself and became obedient to death—even death on a cross!
—Philippians 2:8 NIV

RECENTLY MY CHURCH presented a musical production to celebrate the Christmas season. We had elves and wooden toy soldiers and even Santa himself. We had a singing Christmas tree, soloists from around the country, dance troupes, and lots of Christmas carols. The actors portrayed what life might have been like when Jesus was living, and they even acted out some of the most famous scenes from the Bible. From my spot inside the tree, I had the opportunity to watch the drama night after night. For five performances I watched as Jesus was born, wise men came, and angels sang. I watched night after night as an angry mob beat Jesus bloody and hung him on a cross to die.

I know they were actors and what I was witnessing was not real. As a Christian, I found it difficult not to be transported to that time and place and put myself in the shoes of the mourners. In the shoes of the executioners.

During the past six months, there have been a couple of specific things in my life that God has called me to do. Instead of responding with immediate compliance, I continued to pray for God to answer me. I continued asking him to make it clear to me what I am to do in and about specific situations. And all the while his answer remained the same. Normally I am quick to obey. I *want* God's favor. I desire God's blessing in my life and I look for ways I can obey him and do so in a hurry. But truthfully, with those couple of things, I didn't like what he was telling me. I didn't like the road he had chosen for me. So I kept praying and hoped I was hearing him wrong.

My guess is that Jesus didn't want to be beaten and tortured and then killed in such a public, shameful way. The Bible tells us that Jesus was fully human *and* fully God. I can't think of any reason a human being would desire to endure that kind of pain and misery.

And that's the thing: he didn't want it. *That's not what it is about.* Wanting the circumstances that come our way is not what life's about. Jesus went to the cross because that is what God told him to do. Our focus is all wrong. Instead of looking around us, we need to be fully focused on God. Whatever he sends our way we need to trust him that he has a plan—The Plan—and that plan is always perfect.

The image of that actor hanging on the cross will be in my mind for a long time. It had nothing to do with the cross, yet it had *everything* to do with the cross. Jesus wanted to please his heavenly Father more than he wanted anything else on this earth. Do you? Do you know him? Are you quick to obey him? Take a minute now and ask God to help you follow him no matter what.

PETER AND
THE BOAT

> But Peter said, "Lord, if it's you, tell me to come to you on the water."
> Peter got down out of the boat, walked on the water and came toward
> Jesus. But when he saw the wind, he was afraid and, beginning to
> sink, cried out, "Lord, save me!"
>
> —Matthew 14:28-31 NIV

D O YOU EVER feel like you are in a dark place and can't see your
way out? Or that the light at the end of the tunnel is actually a
train coming your way? Some days are like that.

Let's talk about a man named Peter. He was a follower of Jesus and
loved him very much. Peter was not a perfect man; he was just like you
and me.

One day, Peter and his friends were out in their boat fishing. To prove
a point, Jesus missed them before they left shore. To catch up with them,
he literally walked on the surface of the water out to the boat. Well, a
storm was brewing and Peter and his friends were afraid. In addition
to that, they saw a figure walking on the water. They thought it was a
ghost, actually, because it was the middle of the night. Peter wanted to
walk out to Jesus, so Jesus told him to come ahead. Partway through,
Peter started sinking.

Here's the thing about that story. *Peter walked on the surface of the
water just like Jesus.* Jesus made that happen. But as soon as Peter took

his eyes off Jesus and started looking at his surroundings, he saw the wind and the waves and was scared.

This is such a profound passage. What is God wanting to do in your life and in your heart that you are too afraid to trust him with? What circumstances are you in that have taken your focus from God and put them on your surroundings? Take some time right now to talk with God about all that's on your heart.

THE LION

Stay alert; be in prayer so you don't wander into temptation without even knowing you're in danger.

—Matthew 26:40 NIV

THIS VERSE REALLY jumped off the page at me. The Bible talks about Satan as a lion that is wandering around the earth, just looking for someone to eat. Scary, eh? The hard part is that grief and sadness sometimes cloud our vision without us realizing it. I'm pretty slow sometimes, and this is definitely an area where I struggle. Everything can seem fine, then bad stuff starts happening. Stuff like not getting a good night's rest or being late for an appointment. Little stuff. Then it builds from there until I find myself overly emotional about simple stuff. That's usually when it hits me that something is going on.

For me, I wrestle with my thoughts. I woke up one morning thinking about an old boyfriend. An old, *old* boyfriend. All of the sudden I was going to call him and find out how he was doing. It made perfect sense in my reality. But then I got really suspicious of myself. Why was I suddenly so interested in finding him? When I stepped back, I realized that I was in the midst of an emotionally charged holiday season and some unacknowledged grief.

The first part of that verse tells us to *stay alert*. Satan knows his best chance to break us down and discourage us further is when we already have a head start. If we are distracted by our grief and sadness and not aware of what is going on around us, we make his job much easier.

Take some time now to think about if you are staying alert. I know this may be a time of pain and grief and sadness for you. Don't compound it with bad choices or letting the enemy tell you lies. Write down three ways the enemy beats you down and discourages you. Then ask God to help you recognize those lies for what they are and overcome them with the truth of God's word.

FRIENDS

The religion scholars and Pharisees are competent teachers in God's Law. You won't go wrong in following their teachings on Moses. But be careful about following them. They talk a good line, but they don't live it. They don't take it into their hearts and live it out in their behavior. It's all spit-and-polish veneer.

—Matthew 23:2-3

MY MOM USED to tell me to be careful who my friends were. She said that she could tell the kind of person I was by who I hung around with. That never made any sense to me. Who cares who my friends were? I always thought it was her attempt to control me. What a shock to find out as I got older how right she was! It has been surprising to me in my adult life to see what an influence friends can have on my life. Is it because I'm weaker than other people that I succumb to peer pressure more easily? I don't know. What I do know is how careful I have become about friend selection.

Let me give you an example. I know lots of people in the different circles of my life. Some of them are very close to me, and I would not hesitate to ask their opinion in a personal matter. But in other relationships, I would never ask for advice or guidance on a very important issue. Is it because I think they're stupid? No. I know a lot of well-educated, smart people. I have just become careful about whose advice I'm willing to listen to.

Jesus talked about this in the book of Matthew. He was talking about a group of religious leaders, seen by many to be educated and knowledgeable. Jesus told the people that their factual information was correct, but that was about it. In other words, they looked good, but they may not have been living out what they said was right and true.

Who in your life does this apply to? Does it apply to you? Do you look good on the outside, saying all the right things, but your heart is not where it should be? Ask Jesus to come into your heart today and cleanse you from the inside out.

A MATTER OF
PRIORITIES

Do not store up for yourselves treasures on earth, where moth and rust destroy, and where thieves break in and steal. But store up for yourselves treasures in heaven where moth and rust do not destroy and where thieves do not break in and steal. For where your treasure is, there your heart will be also.

—Matthew 6:19-21 NIV

WHAT IS MOST important to you? Take a minute to think on those things. What do you spend most of your time during the day doing? On what do you spend your money? These two questions alone will help get you started. There is no wrong answer to this exercise. Just think about it for a minute.

Now for the harder question. Do your answers to the above questions match what you *think* your priorities are? What you *say* they are? Priorities are hard. It's easy to deceive ourselves.

In the Bible, Jesus was teaching the people one afternoon. He told them not to store up earthly treasures, but to store up treasures in heaven. What is he talking about in these verses? Material things eventually break down. Moths eat through our favorite sweaters, our ipods will eventually stop working or be replaced by something new and different. A thief can take our money or our possessions. But the treasures we have stored up in our heart, things like love, hope, and peace, can never be taken away from us. Sure, we can have a bad day or

Satan can discourage us, but no one can take those things away from us like they can material things.

What is important to you? I mean *really* important. Take a minute to write about what you really want your life to look like. Sure, we all want more money or a bigger place to live or a nicer car, but those are not the things that bring peace or happiness. They are nice for a while, but eventually they break down and we are subjected to the same old empty feeling again. For me, I would rather have peace in my life than any material thing. That's something that can never be taken away.

A WOMAN LIKE MARY

> The angel went to her and said, "Greetings, you who are highly favored! The Lord is with you." Mary was greatly troubled at his words and wondered what kind of greeting this might be. But the angel said to her, "Do not be afraid, Mary; you have found favor with God. You will conceive and give birth to a son, and you are to call him Jesus.
>
> —Luke 1:28-31

WE'RE ALL FAMILIAR with the Christmas story. Mary gets pregnant and has a baby who turns out to be Jesus. The shepherds come from far and wide to the stable where Jesus was born. The wise men bring gifts of gold, frankincense, and myrrh. Sound familiar?

Did you know that Mary had a crisis pregnancy? Imagine being in her shoes. She felt the same shame and guilt without doing anything to bring it on. She could have aborted her baby. She could have abandoned her baby. She could have freaked out and not trusted God with whatever his plan was for her and her child.

But she *chose* to trust God. Do you remember what it felt like when you first found out you were pregnant? I hardly remember anything from those days. It was like a cloud had settled over me and my life and I was in the fog. Here I was in the middle of the decisions I had made and I was *not* happy. I wanted to die. I thought about killing myself, but I was too afraid. I wanted to run. But run where? Being pregnant isn't like anything else. I couldn't just walk away from it. It was happening inside of me!

We don't read about Mary freaking out in any of these ways. She just quietly trusted God to make sense out of the mess. Are you willing to do that? Are you willing to give God whatever mess is in your life today, at this moment, and trust him with it? Take a moment to reflect on this right now. Ask God to give you courage to trust him through the mess.

A MAN LIKE JOSEPH

The birth of Jesus took place like this. His mother, Mary, was engaged to be married to Joseph. Before they came to the marriage bed, Joseph discovered she was pregnant. (It was by the Holy Spirit, but he didn't know that.) Joseph, chagrined but noble, determined to take care of things quietly so Mary would not be disgraced.

—Matthew 1:18-19

B ACK IN THOSE days, engagement was a much bigger deal than it is today. Being engaged in Mary's day was very serious. So serious, in fact, that they would have had to divorce in order to call off the engagement. They were legally bound to each other, but not yet living together as husband and wife. Joseph finds out that Mary is pregnant, and he hasn't even slept with her yet. He must have been steamed! But instead of making a fuss, "Joseph determined to take care of things quietly so Mary would not be disgraced." He was going to divorce her, but quietly, without anyone else knowing.

Divorce was Joseph's absolute right. He was supposed to marry a virgin, and Mary *was* a virgin. Or that's what he thought. When he found out otherwise, he was allowed to divorce her. But he didn't want her to be disgraced. He cared about her feelings.

How many of your guys stood beside you throughout your pregnancy? How many went to appointments with you and looked at family profiles with you? How many of your boyfriends called and wrote letters of support while you were sacrificing your body and your comfort and your lifestyle to carry and deliver a child you were never going to parent? If you had one who stood by you, consider yourself lucky. The statistics for guys who stick around when their girlfriend gets pregnant are very low. And in the age of "hooking up," what is a boyfriend, anyway?

Here's the point. Joseph wasn't like that. He had grounds to leave Mary, but he didn't. Instead, he, like Mary, chose to trust God. Joseph is an example of Jesus to us. He did the right thing in spite of difficult circumstances. My challenge to you today is to keep trusting God despite what is going on around you. Take a moment and ask God to give you the strength to do just that.

STORIES FROM JESUS

Listen. What do you make of this? A farmer planted seed. As he scattered the seed, some of it fell on the road and birds ate it. Some fell in the gravel; it sprouted quickly but didn't put down roots, so when the sun came up it withered just as quickly. Some fell in the weeds; as it came up, it was strangled among the weeds and nothing came of it. Some fell on good earth and came up with a flourish, producing a harvest exceeding his wildest dreams.

—Mark 1:3-8

ONE OF THE things I love so much about the Bible is the stories like the one above. Jesus was able to convey spiritual meaning using stories that involved just about anything. I like that because sometimes I don't "get it" right away and a story can help me visualize the true meaning.

In this passage, Jesus is trying to make his followers understand why not everyone becomes a Christian. The scattering of the seed represents God's Word going out to people everywhere. This can be in the form of church attendance, or one person telling another person about Jesus, or a missionary sharing with someone who does not know about God.

Once the seed is spread, there are four possibilities. In the first case, the seed is put down and right away Satan comes and snatches it away. Satan does not want you or me or anyone to believe in Jesus.

The second choice is that a person hears about Jesus and is excited but doesn't "put down roots." In other words, the person is filled with joy at the knowledge of God but doesn't go to church, doesn't go to a Bible study, doesn't even open a Bible. Because they have no roots, they wither and their joy dies out.

The third choice is that the person hears about God and receives him into their life. But the "weeds" strangle out the message. The weeds refer to the worries of their lives or their preoccupation with wealth. These things get in the way of their new-found belief in God and chokes it until it goes away.

Finally, the fourth choice is that the seed falls onto good soil, sprouts roots, has no weeds in its way, and grows healthy and strong.

Which one are you? I remember times in my life when I was the second one. I went to a camp or a church service and got excited about God, but I didn't have any roots to keep that excitement alive. It took many times before the seed fell into the good soil of my heart, was cultivated, put down good roots, and grew. Take heart if you are struggling today. Don't be discouraged. Ask God to remove any weed or obstacle that is in your way of getting to know him better.

JESUS FEEDS
5,000 PEOPLE

Jesus got them all to sit down in groups of fifty or a hundred—they looked like a patchwork quilt of wildflowers spread out on the green grass! He took the five loaves and two fish, lifted his face to heaven in prayer, blessed, broke, and gave the bread to the disciples, and the disciples in turn gave it to the people. He did the same with the fish. They all ate their fill. The disciples gathered twelve baskets of leftovers. More than five thousand were at the supper.

—Mark 6:39-44

THIS IS ONE of the most famous stories from the Bible. You have probably heard it even if you have never been to church. Jesus and his followers were trying to get away to have a break from all the people. But the people saw them leaving town and followed after them. Do you ever wonder why people were so drawn to Jesus? I think it's because he loved them and cared about them no matter what their station in life. He loved the leper, the tax collector, and the prostitute. It didn't matter to Jesus then, and it doesn't matter to him now. He loves you and me just how we are, no matter where we are.

All these people followed Jesus, and he started teaching them. The disciples tried to get Jesus to send the people away because it was getting late in the day. They knew everyone was going to be hungry, and they were probably getting hungry themselves. But instead, Jesus challenged his disciples to feed the people. They thought Jesus was crazy! Did he know how much it would cost to feed all these people?

The disciples asked among the people and found five loaves of bread and two fish. Jesus took it, lifted it up to heaven, and thanked God for it. Then he had the disciples pass it around to all the people. The Bible says that they all ate until they were full! When the disciples picked up the crumbs of bread left over, they too ate until they were full. The last verse refers to five thousand people, but that was only counting the men. Women and children were never included in counts. So it may have been more than ten thousand people!

What are you thinking after reading this? What is going on in your life that you are afraid to trust God with? If God can feed those people with a few loaves of bread and some fish, surely he can fix whatever is wrong in your life. Take a minute today to express your need for God.

SUFFERING

Don't run from suffering; embrace it. Follow me and I'll show you how. Self-help is no help at all. Self-sacrifice is the way, my way, to saving yourself, your true self. What good would it do to get everything you want and lose you, the real you? What could you ever trade your soul for?

—Mark 8:35-37

WHEN I WAS very young, my mom taught Vacation Bible School at our church over the summer. Back then, Bible school was two weeks long, a very long time when handling lots of little children. My sister and I thought we were special because my mom was one of the teachers which meant we got all the music and lyrics ahead of time. By the time it started, my sister and I knew all the words to all the songs. We thought it was neat. It made us feel grown up.

One year we did one of *Psalty's Kids' Praise* curriculums. The above verse was one of the key verses for the whole two weeks. I remember hearing about denying myself and picking up my cross, but I didn't know what that meant.

As I grew older, I started understanding a little more at a time. Then during my pregnancy, I learned a lot about suffering. That was a very pivotal time in my life. But it was also a very important time in my spiritual development. I had grown up in church, attended Sunday school, Bible school, and church functions, but I had never internalized the fact that Jesus came to earth as a man and was murdered for *me*. It wasn't just some story that was made up to make Easter more meaningful or Christmas more joyful. It really happened, and if I had been the only one on this planet, God would have still come and died for me so I could spend eternity in heaven.

The end of that verse asks us what on this earth would be worth trading our soul for. A good question. What in your life is worth dying for? What good is it if we gain the whole world and all its riches and pleasures yet give away our soul? Jesus made us to be eternal creatures. This life is not the end. Take a minute now and reflect on these thoughts.

CHILDREN

The people brought children to Jesus, hoping he might touch them. The disciples shooed them off. But Jesus was irate and let them know it: "Don't push these children away. Don't ever get between them and me. These children are at the very center of life in the kingdom. Mark this: Unless you accept God's kingdom in the simplicity of a child, you'll never get in." Then, gathering the children up in his arms, he laid his hands of blessing on them.

—Mark 10:13-6

J ESUS LOVES CHILDREN. It's true. This passage proves it. Your decision for the life of your unborn child touched the heart of God. I know it was more than likely the hardest choice to make, but God knows that and will bless you for it.

The other thing this passage tells us is how we are to approach God and spiritual things. We are not supposed to be mature, all-knowing, educated beings. He wants us to come to him like a child. If you don't currently have small children in your home, let's think about that. My little girl is full of wonder about the world around her. She uses all of her senses to experience that world. She hears the faint sound of the passing train, or the song of a bird. She has to touch things for herself. She is starting to notice the scents as the trees bloom and the flowers bud. She uses her eyes to look at the green grass and the wind blowing in the trees. And finally, she is learning to put words to all of these new experiences.

This is how God wants us to approach him—in wide-eyed wonder, like a child experiencing spring for the first time. Like a child trusts their parent to lead them and guide them and care for them. That's how God wants us to trust him.

Where is your level of trust today? Take a minute and reflect on it. Ask God to help you trust him more and more.

ASK GOD

Jesus was matter-of-fact: "Embrace this God-life. Really embrace it, and nothing will be too much for you. This mountain, for instance: Just say, 'Go jump in the lake'...and it's as good as done. That's why I urge you to pray for absolutely everything, ranging from small to large. Include everything as you embrace this God-life, and you'll get God's everything. And when you assume the posture of prayer, remember that it's not all asking. If you have anything against someone, forgive—only then will your heavenly Father be inclined to also wipe your slate clean of sins."

—Mark 11:22-25

JESUS IS TALKING about our prayer life in this passage. He is explaining the powerful effects prayer can have for the believer. He tells us that if we believe, anything is possible. We can even command a mountain to jump into the ocean!

God wants to bless us and see us successful. The trick is that it is not all about us and what we *want*. It is about God and trusting him to provide for what we *need*. This requires us to look beyond ourselves and our circumstances and connect with the one who created us in the first place.

No matter where you are right now, God wants to connect with your heart. He wants you to tell him what is going on in your life and what you think you need. He also wants the opportunity to speak to you concerning what he has for you. He wants the opportunity to change your heart.

I was recently feeling overwhelmed with everything going on in my life. I spent some of my prayer time explaining to God all my responsibilities and commitments, and then I asked him to remove some of them. After waiting, God once again showed me that I was supposed to be involved in everything on my plate. Not only did he change my heart attitude about the situation, but he added another activity! If I had followed my own plan and cut out one of my commitments, I may have cut off God from working in an area of my life.

Where are you today? Feeling overwhelmed? Lost? Confused? God can fix all of that. Spend a few minutes in prayer with him. If it helps, write down your prayers so you can refer to them later, when God starts working in your heart and changing you.

SATISFACTION

I have learned to be content whatever the circumstances...
—Philippians 4:11 NIV

ARE YOU SATISFIED with your life? Are you happy with where you are emotionally, physically, and spiritually?

There's a guy named Paul in the Bible. He is known for writing several of its books, including Philippians. Paul was a missionary; he traveled around and told people about God. In this particular letter, he talks about the joy he has at his opportunities to spread the gospel of Jesus Christ.

The only thing is...Paul is in *jail* as he is writing this letter. My guess is that going to jail in Paul's time was not like going to jail in our time. Nowadays, a prisoner gets a bed and three square meals a day. Prisons in Paul's day were dark, smelly, and probably rat-infested. Prisoners were either chained to the wall or chained to a prison guard. This was not your modern-day jail.

Paul had obviously learned the secret of being happy. In the movie *City Slickers*, Curly tells Billy Crystal's character that the true meaning of happiness is one thing. Billy Crystal cannot wait to find out what that is. But Curly says, "You have to figure it out for yourself. It's different for everyone."

Obviously, jail does not seem like it would make anyone happy. But Paul was not looking at his circumstances. He found what gave him joy,

226

and he was doing it. He didn't care that it had landed him in jail. Paul wrote to his friends that he had learned to be content.

Are you looking at your circumstances today? Are you at peace despite the turmoil all around you? Take a minute and reflect on where you are today.

LEAN ON ME

Cast all your anxiety on him because he cares for you.

—1 Peter 5:7 NIV

I HAVE LEARNED how to lean on Jesus. I remember three events in the fairly recent past where I was confronted with an emergency situation in my own life. My immediate reaction in all three situations was to call my husband. As God would have it, he was not available; in fact, in one situation, he was physically far away on a business trip.

In all three situations, I thought I needed someone stronger than me to hold my hand and walk me through the coming storm. I was right. What was wrong was the *who* I needed.

I mistakenly thought that since God had given me a man, a husband, a priest of my home, that he was who I needed to turn to in times of greatest need. The truth is that God wants us to rely on him. Single or married, whatever phase of life we are in, he wants us to come to him and allow him to provide for us. Notice I said *allow* him to provide for us. He loves us and wants the best for us; of course he's going to take care of us. But we have to allow him the opportunity.

In one situation, I needed immediate medical attention at the emergency room. I could not transport myself and I thought my husband should take me. But he wasn't available. So I had no choice but to allow God to provide for me. And he did. My work associate graciously drove me to the hospital and then home going many miles out of her way.

Where do you go first when you are faced with a crisis? Do you turn to your friends? Your parents? God wants us to turn to him first. He wants us to trust him enough to provide for us. He loves you, created you, and will never leave you, especially in your time of need. Won't you trust him today?

Take a minute and think of a time when you went to someone besides God first. Now, rewrite that situation and go to God first. How hard would that be to do next time?

TRIALS

Consider it a sheer gift, friends, when tests and challenges come at you from all sides. You know that under pressure, your faith-life is forced into the open and shows its true colors. So don't try to get out of anything prematurely. Let it do its work so you become mature and well-developed, not deficient in any way…Anyone who meets a testing challenge head-on and manages to stick it out is mighty fortunate. For such persons loyally in love with God, the reward is life and more life.

—James 1:2-4, 12

I DON'T KNOW about you, but when something challenging is going on in my life, my automatic response is not to cheer and jump up and down. My first response is often "Why?" or "Seriously, haven't I been through enough?" Good attitude, right?

God sees challenges differently. We should consider challenges a gift? A gift when bad things happen? Or when things stop going the right way? Is he *crazy*? But keep reading. It is only through trials that we learn to persevere. Webster defines "persevere" as *maintaining a purpose in spite of difficulty, obstacles, or discouragement.*

Does this describe you? Where are you today? Take time right now to write in your journal about what you are persevering in your life this day. Is it a trial? A disappointment? Tell God about it right now.

TEMPTATION

When tempted, no one should say, "God is tempting me." For God cannot be tempted by evil, nor does he tempt anyone; but each one is tempted when, by his own evil desire, he is dragged away and enticed.

—James 1:13-14 NIV

SATAN HAS NOTHING better to do with his time than watch you and know what your weaknesses are. He spends every waking moment watching you and waiting to see if he needs to take you out. If you are living life for yourself and have no interest in God, then Satan has no interest in you.

But if you have accepted Jesus into your heart and are trying to live for him by going to church, reading your Bible, and doing the right thing, then look out. You are one of Satan's targets.

I can be going along fine, driving in my car, listening to the radio, when suddenly out of nowhere this discouraging voice starts saying, "Your house isn't big enough. You deserve so much better. How come your husband makes you stay in a house that is bursting at the seams?"

My immediate thought is this is Satan's invitation to derail me. While I don't consider myself materialistic, I would love a bigger house with a different floor plan. But these words whispered in my ear are trying to tempt me to pour my time and energy into pursuing that elusive dream house instead of doing the things God has called me to do, like write this book.

God has provided for my every need in my current house. We are warm, safe, and dry. What else do we need? I know better than to think that God is behind this temptation.

What are you struggling with today? What temptation is in your life disguised as something else? Take time to recognize those things and thank God for helping you see them for what they are.

LISTENING AND DOING

Don't fool yourself into thinking that you are a listener when you are anything but, letting the Word go in one ear and out the other. Act on what you hear! Those who hear and don't act are like those who glance in the mirror, walk away, and two minutes later have no idea who they are, what they look like.

—James 1:22-24

WHEN I WAS a child, my mother used to tell me I had selective hearing. Whenever I heard that I would think, "Gee, my hearing is fine. I hear everything. I wonder what she means by that?"

Of course, now I know. My mother, for some reason, thought I only heard what I wanted to hear. I wonder why she thought that. Maybe because I would only do the things I wanted to do. If she asked me to do a list of things, I would pick out the ones I felt like doing and leave the rest undone.

According to the verse above, I was not a good listener. When it comes to being followers of God, we cannot have selective hearing. It's true some churches and some religions choose the things they like about the Bible and follow only those things. They forget about everything else. However, *all* of the Bible is important. ALL of it is given to us by God for our own self-improvement. Therefore, whatever we read we must apply. The only way to do that is to ask God to help us understand it.

What do you think about that? Take a minute to write your thoughts and reactions in your journal. Ask God to help you be a better listener and doer.

WORDS

It only takes a spark, remember, to set off a forest fire. A careless or wrongly placed word out of your mouth can do that. By our speech we can ruin the world, turn harmony to chaos, throw mud on a reputation, send the whole world up in smoke and go up in smoke with it, smoke right from the pit of hell.

—James 3:5-6

THIS PAST LENTEN season (the time between Ash Wednesday and Easter), I decided to give up something unusual. I felt convicted that maybe I wasn't speaking as respectfully as I could to others. This included everybody in my circle of influence: family, friends, children, and acquaintances. I can often be very sarcastic, and while that may be funny to some people, others can be offended by it. So, in all areas of my life, I decided to really pay special attention to how I talked and the language I used.

Now, I don't normally use profanities, but when I get upset, that is another matter. So, at the time, that wasn't really my issue. I just wanted to make sure I was speaking respectfully to those around me.

Did you know that your words are powerful? Words can create and build up and encourage. But according to James, they can have a devastating effect as well. What a responsibility we have with our words.

Take a minute and reflect on your words. Do you speak words of love, respect, and caring to your family? Friends? Co-workers? Or are you quick to condemn and "throw mud"? Ask God to help you tame your tongue.

SUBMIT

So let God work his will in you. Yell a loud "no" to the Devil and watch him scamper. Say a quiet "yes" to God and he'll be there in no time. Quit dabbling in sin. Purify your inner life. Quit playing the field. Hit bottom, and cry your eyes out. The fun and games are over. Get serious, really serious. Get down on your knees before the Master; it's the only way you'll get on your feet.

—James 4:7-10

AMAZING WORDS, AND they are right out of the Bible! Who knew God's Word was so relevant to our lives today? God wants us to submit to him—a scary word in our society. Webster defines "submit" this way: *to give over or yield to the power or authority of another*. To give over? Like I'm not in control any longer? Exactly. God wants to have total control over our lives. I know how scary that sounds, but let me explain.

Here on earth, when someone wants to have total control over our lives, it's usually not a good thing. In fact, it is never a good thing. I have almost total control over my twenty-month-old's life, but that is different. And she *still* says no to some things. There are some guys that try and take that control from us as women. But they have wrong motives. I'm talking about as adults in our right minds giving ourselves over to another person…God.

God has nothing but our best interests in mind. He knows that our only hope of a better life is to give ourselves over to him and his plan for us. I know it sounds crazy. But his plans are for our hope and our future. He has plans to prosper us and never to harm us. This isn't the gospel of prosperity, but rather the promise that God will always be there, no matter what life throws at us.

Take a minute and reflect on that. What does that look like in your life? What does that mean to you? Is it a scary thought? Ask God to help you choose him more and more.

THE CHOICE

You adulterous people, don't you know that friendship with the world is hatred toward God? Anyone who chooses to be a friend of the world becomes an enemy of God. Or do you think Scripture says without reason that the spirit he caused to live in us envies intensely?
—James 4:4-6 NIV

IN CASE YOU haven't noticed, the culture we're living in is not exactly God-friendly. The popular media throws around a lot of religious words and phrases. But the truth is that if someone calls themselves a Christian, they are looked down on. Of course, any *other* religion is okay. Tom Cruise and John Travolta claim scientology as their religion. Madonna spouts kaballah. And there are many others. But the truth is those claims are empty. Those religions do not worship the one true Christ, the only one to come back from the dead.

The world and Christianity are far apart. James wrote a letter to Jewish Christians around AD 60. That was many years ago, as we are living in the 21st century now. It is amazing how his comments to those people apply to our own culture today.

You have a choice to make. Are you going to be friends with this world? Or are you going to be friends with God? Take a minute and write your thoughts. How does this relate to you and your life? Do you need to change anything? Ask God to help you. Are you already on the right track? Ask God to encourage you.

NO OTHER GOD

Oh yes, you shaped me first inside, then out; you formed me in my mother's womb. I thank you, High God—you're breathtaking! Body and soul, I am marvelously made!...You know me inside and out, you know every bone in my body; You know exactly how I was made, bit by bit, how I was sculpted from nothing into something. Like an open book, you watched me grow from conception to birth.

—Psalm 139:13-16

I CAN'T LET an opportunity pass by to brag about God's faithfulness in my life. I never thought I would see this day come. Twenty years is a long time! I am so blessed by God's continued patience with me, his working in my heart to clean it and restore it to something that can actually be used.

He promises us new mercies every single morning. No matter what we have done, no matter how far we have strayed, all we have to do is ask God to cleanse us and forgive us and take us back. And he *does*!

No other religion can boast a God like mine. No other religion worships a god who can see and hear, and who cares about the intricacies of my daily life. He knows the number of hairs on my head. He created me and formed my innermost being.

What a happy day! I'm going to take today and just think about all the things God has done in my life over twenty years. I am truly not the same person I was.

Claim this day as your own personal day of thanksgiving. What has God done for you? List your blessings and thank him for each one.

TAKING BACK WHAT BELONGS TO GOD

All day long my enemies taunt me; those who rail against me use my name as a curse.

—Psalm 102:8 NIV

MY HUSBAND AND I love action movies. Recently we watched *The Bourne Ultimatum*. The fast pace of the scenes left us breathless with excitement. It felt like we were actually in the film! If you are familiar with this movie, you know that the main character, Jason Bourne, has lost his memory and is seeking to figure out who he is. He has been mentally reprogrammed to be an assassin.

Toward the end of the movie, someone finally tells him what his name used to be. While he still doesn't remember everything, he begins to remember bits and pieces of his life and his nature before the bad guys took control of him.

After the movie, I was left shaking my head and wondering. Isn't that what the enemy of our souls is trying to do to us? Satan does not want us living for God, claiming victory and living a life that is useful and purposeful. He wants us to stay stuck in our sin, our shame, and our guilt. Making a decision to follow Jesus doesn't mean we are always moving forward. Maybe Satan can't make us engage in our old activities, but he can sure keep us stuck by reminding us of them over and over and over.

At the end of the movie, Bourne goes to the main bad guy and takes his name back. He renounces the name Jason Bourne and reclaims his old name.

Jesus created you from nothing. He formed you inside your mother's womb before she even knew she was pregnant. He knows the whole plan for your life. He already knows your mistakes and your victories from the time you were born until the day you die. There is nothing you can do that will surprise him. Yet you and you alone have the power to choose. You have the ability to choose if you are going to follow God or not.

If you have decided to follow God, your next challenge is to take back who God intended you to be. God named you Redeemed, Precious, Beautiful, Apple of his eye. Satan wants you to keep the name of Liar, Murderer, Adulteress, and Thief.

I challenge you the next time Satan whispers in your ear and reminds you of all the bad stuff you've done to speak out and renounce him. Start telling him who you really are in Christ. Take back who God intended you to be. Stand strong on God's promises and watch what he begins to do in your life.

EXPERIENCE IS EVERYTHING

A farmer went out to sow his seed…As he was scattering the seed, some fell on rocky places, where it did not have much soil. It sprang up quickly, because the soil was shallow. But when the sun came up, the plants were scorched, and they withered because they had no root.
—Matthew 13:3, 5-6 NIV

A RECENT AD for men's cologne carried the tag line "Experience is everything." Judging from the television commercial, the experience they are referring to is probably not the same thing the Bible talks about.

We live in a pop culture, where teens become superstars overnight. Athletes are drafted into pro sports right out of high school and college. And new believers in Christ are propelled into leadership in the church. What's wrong with this picture?

To put it plainly, *experience* is what's missing. I love the zealous nature of new believers. It's contagious. It's exciting to watch as they grasp more and more of God's love for them and the plan he has for their lives. It's awesome to be around them to remind us of how exciting it is to come to know Jesus. The missing piece is experience.

Think of it like a small child. How cool is it to be around a toddler as she grasps her world and begins to see how it works? How neat is it to watch her figure out that she can change the color of something with a crayon? But is she ready to teach others how to use a crayon? Is she ready to teach others how to read? Of course not. She doesn't have the maturity or the experience necessary to teach someone else how to do these things.

The same is true of new believers. Their excitement is awesome, but that is not what carries them. Having an experience with God day after day, week after week, month after month, year after year on good days and bad days, through happy times and sad times is what I'm talking about. That is what is going to carry them through. The excitement of a new relationship with Christ jumpstarts us, but it's the day-in-day-out faithfulness on our part that establishes good roots and sustains the relationship.

Experience is everything because it helps us establish roots, which helps us grow even stronger in our faith. Where are you today? Is your relationship with Christ going to fade away when the hard times come because you have no root and only excitement? Get grounded by finding a Bible-believing church home. Read the Bible for yourself. Memorize verses so that when the hard days come you will be sustained.

IMAGE IS EVERYTHING

They exchanged their Glory for an image of a bull, which eats grass. They forgot the God who saved them...

—Psalm 106:20-21 NIV

THERE IS NO doubt that we live in an image-driven society. As consumers, we base our buying choices—like the cars we drive, the clothes we wear, the food we eat, and even the church we attend—on image and appearance. We look at the packaging to tell us if the message is even worth listening to. If the image is acceptable, we are more likely to try it out. Because we have become so visually oriented as a society, we have developed a distaste for anything that is not shiny, new, modern, and current. I especially believe this is true when it comes to our churches.

How many of us have sacrificed content at church in exchange for shiny, flashy monitors, up-tempo praise bands, and new buildings? How many of our pastors are on television or the internet now? If your pastor isn't, how do you feel about that?

We have to be careful. Just because something *looks* good doesn't mean it *is* good. Think of Snow White. The apple she ate was pretty and no doubt shiny. But it was poisonous. Compare that to celebrities. They look happy and healthy, like they have it all together. But in reality many are addicted to drugs, cheating on their spouses and empty inside. We have to be very careful what image we buy into and how we let images affect us and our choices.

The verse above refers to the slaves in Egypt, whom God himself rescued and set free. They had been enslaved for a very long time when God freed them. Yet they quickly forgot all he had done for them. Instead of praising and worshipping a supernatural God who had worked miracle after miracle on their behalf, they desired a physical god that they could touch and see. So they made a calf out of their gold jewelry. A calf is a creation of God who eats grass. God is a creation of no one and doesn't require food or drink or rest.

Which would you rather have? A god made out of gold that can neither see nor hear nor speak? Or a God who created you and planned for you from the beginning of time, one who knows your every move and every care and is with you all the time, in every situation? Take a minute now to ask God to remove the veil from your eyes so you can see things for what they really are.

WOMAN

So that they will wisely train the young women to be sane and sober of mind (temperate, disciplined) and to love their husbands and their children, to be self-controlled, chaste, homemakers, good-natured (kindhearted), adapting and subordinating themselves to their husbands, that the word of God may not be exposed to reproach (blasphemed or discredited).

—Titus 2:4-5

SO MUCH FOR the modern day, independent woman, eh? What a great passage. Actually, these words have caused me much consternation in my young life. The desire deep in my heart is to walk more closely with God, to know him better, to know more deeply what it means to be a woman and a wife and a mother, and all the things that I am. The problem is that the church seems to be in short supply of women truly willing to mentor other women. The older generation had good solid mentoring: the women got together regularly. They quilted and talked and cooked together. Visiting was an important part of their lives and culture, not a luxury they afforded themselves when they caught up on laundry.

What happened? What changed? I wish I knew. I wish I understood why for so many years I have been repeatedly let down by the older women in my church. I suppose part of it is my fault. I have expected the women to care about the next generation and have a desire in their hearts to mentor me and teach me what it means to be a woman. But I have yet to find her.

A few years ago, in my endless quest to connect with a more experienced woman, I joined a group at my church specifically for moms and mentors. My assumption was that the more experienced women would be mentoring the younger, newer moms. Again, I was disappointed. I don't understand why the older women are too busy to do their biblical duty in mentoring the younger generation.

Here's what I think: Our culture and society have become very individual-focused. It used to be the family unit that was important, but now it seems all that's important is me, me, me. We see it everywhere, and it is becoming more and more evident in technology. We have individual email accounts, individual cell phones. Gone are the days of the family road trip or even sitting on the front porch. Now when a family takes a road trip, each person has an ipod, a personal DVD player, or their own hand-held video game. Instead of connecting with one another, we are each into our own thing.

I don't think this is how it's supposed to be. We were made for relationships. Jesus gave us the example of relationship. In fact, the only thing that saves us from eternal punishment is our relationship with God; it's not the religion or even the church attendance. The relationships are what matter.

Further, I think our continual growing comes through relationships. We are commanded to love one another, to overlook each other's offenses and to bear one another's burdens. How can we do that if we are not in relationship with others?

Take a minute and ask God to show you the importance of relationships in your own life. Ask him to help you make relationships more of a priority.

SURRENDER

"I surrender all, I surrender all; All to thee, my blessed Savior, I surrender all."

—Words by Judson W. Van DeVenter, 1896

HAVE YOU EVER been to a church and seen people lifting up their hands in worship? Ever wonder why they do that? Have you ever seen someone give up on something? Maybe they are conceding loss in a game or have worked so hard on something only to see it crumble in front of them. Have you ever seen someone throw up their hands, shrug and say "I just don't get it"? It's all the same thing. Surrender is surrender, whatever the form.

As a believer, there's something very freeing about going to God and saying, "I don't get it." There's something about being able to let go of something and letting God take control. That's what he wants. God's in control of everything anyway, right? So when we come to the end of ourselves, when we come to the place where we can't go forward or backwards or up or down, and the situation seems hopeless, that's when we usually turn to God and hand him the problem. That's what he wants. Maybe he allows us to get frustrated and work ourselves into a corner just so we will surrender. Ever think about it that way?

So, why are we so dead-set on figuring things out for ourselves? Why don't we surrender more? Do we perceive it as a weakness to let go of something and let God take it on and make it work? I think this is one of the biggest challenges of this life. The world is preaching secular humanism, where everything is relevant and you are your own god. They tell us to rely on ourselves and our intellect. The emphasis on college degrees and other degree programs is on the rise. We are more educated than any other generation.

Yet, God calls us to be still and listen to his still, small voice. He promises that if we will build our lives on him, he will make a way for us and have a relationship with us and do things in our lives that are too wonderful to tell. We don't need a college degree for that. In fact, it seems like the more education we have, the more we tend to rely on ourselves and our own intellect. It's kind of like Eve and the fruit. God was enough for her and Adam. God had provided everything they could ever want or need. But Satan lied and convinced her that God wasn't enough. Isn't that the same lie he's feeding us today? *God isn't enough for you. He can't meet all your needs or solve all your problems. You have to take care of yourself. Get education so you can learn how to get what you need.*

Surrender all to God today. He's the only one who truly knows what you need. He's the only one who created you and knows how to care for you.

TEMPORARY COMFORT

Friends, this world is not your home, so don't make yourselves cozy in it. Don't indulge your ego at the expense of your soul. Live an exemplary life among the natives so that your actions will refute their prejudices. Then they'll be won over to God's side and be there to join in the celebration when he arrives.

—1 Peter 2:12

ARE YOU AT home here? Are you comfortable in this life? This can be a challenge whether you are a Christian or not. This life is not the end. It doesn't matter if you believe that or not; it's the truth. So, what does that look like in your life? Passages like these urge us to remember that we are not home yet. We have not arrived at our final destination. We are merely passing through. But seriously, what does this look like? How are we supposed to live and work and make a life here without "getting cozy"?

It takes work, and honestly, it is not always easy. As Christians, we must try and keep an eternal perspective. The test is to manage this one day at a time. Each morning, take time to read the Bible and pray. Ask God what he has in store for you today. Then throughout the day, remind yourself occasionally that you are living for God. Our purpose here is to be a vessel through which God's will can be accomplished. What is happening here and now is not of maximum importance. It's just all a part of God's master plan.

For those of you who have not yet accepted Christ as your personal Lord and Savior, this life seems like all there is. Let me assure you it is not. We were all created to live eternally, not in some reincarnation-type way, but our souls were created to live forever. When this life is over, however long we have, our body will die and be buried in the ground. But our soul will leave our body at the time of death and go to heaven or hell. Yes, these places are real and not merely fairy tales. God has promised us that these places do exist. Heaven is where we will worship God forever and ever. Hell is where we will suffer greatly and forever be separated from God. There will be no more chances to call out to him and accept him in our hearts and lives. He will be removed from our reach forever.

I don't know about you, but being in a place that is forever separated from God is a very scary thought. We may think that our current world is hell on earth sometimes, but believe me, this is nothing compared to what will happen when God is completely removed from the picture. While our world continues to deteriorate now, it is the grace of God that keeps it from spinning madly out of control. According to the Bible, that day is still to come.

If you haven't accepted Christ as your personal Lord and Savior, why haven't you? What is keeping you from making that decision? No one is promised tomorrow. We never know what's going to happen. We don't know when our last breath will come. Our lifetime is a drop of water compared to the ocean of eternity. Won't you invite Jesus to come into your heart and life today?

CONTENTMENT

So be content with who you are, and don't put on airs. God's strong hand is on you; he'll promote you at the right time. Live carefree before God; he is most careful with you.

—I Peter 5:6-7

S ELF-CONFIDENCE. POSITIVE SELF-ESTEEM. Are these things bad? Is there something inherently wrong with feeling good about yourself? Sometimes the Bible seems to tell us not to feel good about ourselves or that it's wrong to do so.

God created us, and we should have a positive view of who we are. Women especially struggle with their appearance and the view they have of themselves and their bodies. We struggle with our self-worth and whether we are valuable on our own without a man. I don't know where this originated, but I'm thinking it may have something to do with the Garden of Eden. Adam and Eve were perfectly comfortable with who they were and who God created them to be. They were naked, but they were not ashamed. However after they eat the fruit, they become ashamed with their nakedness. They then try to cover themselves with fig leaves sewn together. I think we can glean from their mistake. Ever since they ate from the tree of the knowledge of good and evil, men and women have been insecure with how they look.

God is always fighting for us to come back from that place. He wants us to be healthy, whole, and balanced. Part of that is knowing who we are in Christ. It's knowing that we are fearfully and wonderfully made; that we are a pearl of great price; and that he would leave the ninety-nine other sheep just to come and find us and rescue us from where we are.

This verse urges us to be content with who we are and not put on airs. What does that mean? Putting on airs means pretending we are something we are not, or acting like we are more than we actually are. God tells us not to do this because he created us and knows that we are enough the way we are. We don't need to pretend; we only need to press into him and let him fight our battles and make our way for us.

The second part of the verse tells us to live carefree before him. This doesn't mean we get to live any way we want to. Instead, this means we are free to serve God in whatever way he calls us. We are not to be intimidated or limited by this world. Instead of being so careful to live within whatever society has decided is normal, we can be free to live our lives for Christ in whatever way he has called us to do so. If he has called you to serve him overseas or in your own backyard, you have the freedom in Christ to do that without the restraints of this world.

Take a minute and ask God to help you be comfortable in your own skin. Ask him to help you be who he created you to be.

SOWING IN TEARS

And now, GOD, do it again—bring rains to our drought-stricken lives so those who planted their crops in despair will shout hurrahs at the harvest, so those who went off with heavy hearts will come home laughing, with armloads of blessing.

—Psalm 126:4-6

I'VE ALWAYS THOUGHT this verse said something that it doesn't say. The reference in the NIV to "sowing in tears" always gave me the visual of a person bending down over the ground and letting their tears soak into the soil. It sounds really crazy when I say it out loud, but that is the picture that has always been in my mind.

But then I placed my firstborn daughter for adoption.

I clearly remember some of those early experiences after she was born. One time I was shopping with my mother close to Valentine's Day. Just looking at all the heart balloons and happy, cuddly bears made me cry. And the first year of holidays almost sent me over the edge. It was all just too much. The grief, the mixed emotions, and having no one to talk to about any of it.

That's when I started thinking that maybe this verse looks different than I had always pictured it. When I was grieving the loss of my daughter, life didn't stop. As much as I wanted to, I didn't get to stop living. I had to manage school and work and home and all the other things that go along with living. Only now I had to add grief to the mix.

In the Old Testament book of Joshua, the Israelites were destined to take over the Promised Land. The first obstacle keeping them from Canaan was Jericho, a city with big, strong, fortified walls. While the Israelites camped at Gilgal they celebrated Passover. But they also celebrated the rite of circumcision. These were the next generation of Israelites. All but two of the previous generation had died in the desert. But they had not yet been circumcised. Soon after they celebrated this rite, God had them marching around the walls of Jericho for six days. Then on the seventh, they yelled and the walls fell down.

I tell you this because I realized the other day that this is an example of sowing in tears. Did you ever wonder why God had them marching around the walls without saying or doing anything? *Perhaps he was giving them time to heal.* They were sore from the circumcision and unable to fight. But they could march, even stiffly. By the time they were on the seventh day, they were strong and ready for battle. They literally sowed in tears and reaped in victory.

Does any of this apply to your life today? Press in to God and trust what he is doing in your life. He knows your grief and your pain. Nothing is wasted in God's economy.

LOST

Trust in the Lord with all your heart and lean not on your own understanding; in all your ways acknowledge him and he will make your paths straight.

—Proverbs 3:5-6 NIV

HAVE YOU EVER been flying in an airplane in the middle of thick, stormy clouds? Have you ever felt like you were there in your own life? I can remember a time of being in the middle of such a storm.

My birth daughter called me one day with some big news. "I found Chris!" she said excitedly. I had no words. I didn't even know where to begin. Her birth father and I had split long before she was born. I said nothing.

That incident precipitated feelings of loss, confusion, and disorientation in me. For several weeks, I felt like my internal compass was broken. My relationship with God was strained, to say the least. I wrote in my journal that I felt like I was in the middle of the sea, with fog all around me. I couldn't see the shoreline for anything.

Times like that remind me of airplanes. Did you know pilots are trained to fly by their instruments and not by their eyesight? When it's bright, sunny and clear, it's easy to know which way is up, but when the storms move in and the visibility is cut to zero, it all changes. In an airplane surrounded by clouds, pilots can literally not tell which way is up without using their instruments.

This is such an important principle in our spiritual lives. When things are going well, it's easy to see what is good. It's easy to see God's hand on us and our family. It's easy to be full of praise and thanks. But the minute the storm moves in, it's easy to become confused and discouraged.

Our compass for our spiritual lives is the Bible. We cannot merely trust what we see around us. We need the truth of God to illuminate us and show us the way each and every day. God is our breath and our life. Without him we are nothing, nor can we do anything.

Is your compass pointing to true north today? Do you know God personally? Do you see evidence of him in your life? Take a minute right now to adjust your compass. Ask God to remove any fog or anything that is clouding your vision of him.

GREAT IS THY FAITHFULNESS

Great is thy faithfulness, O God my Father; There is no shadow of turning with thee; Thou changest not, they compassions they fail not; As thou hast been, thou forever wilt be. Summer and winter and springtime and harvest; sun, moon and stars in their courses above; Join with all nature in manifold witness, to thy great faithfulness, mercy and love. Pardon for sin and a peace that endureth, thine own dear presence to cheer and to guide; Strength for today and bright hope for tomorrow, Blessings all mine with ten thousand beside.
—Lyrics: Thomas Chisholm, 1923

AS I CLOSE this project, I cannot help but reflect on the long, arduous road. These pages are filled with portions of my journey to find Jesus, find meaning, and find a faith that is rock solid. I haven't always been successful, but I've never given up hope that Jesus can be found and he can make my life worth living.

The words to this classic hymn have expressed my praise in times of thankfulness, brought me peace amidst the storms, and reminded me that no matter the season or time of day, Jesus is always as close as a whisper.

My prayer for you has always been that you would find Jesus, the creator, maker and lover of your soul. No one loves you like he does. He doesn't care how far away you have strayed, what mistakes you have made or how much you have screwed up your life. He loves you and wants you and will take you back in an instant. Commit yourself and your way to him now. Call on him and he will hear you. Let him restore and redeem your life for his glory.

AFTERWORD: KNOWING GOD

I'VE TALKED A lot throughout these pages about knowing God, asking Jesus into your heart and committing your way fully to him. But I couldn't close this project without spelling it out as plain as day. What does it mean to ask Jesus into your heart?

First, you have to admit to God that you are a sinner. Admit that you don't have it all together and that God is your only answer.

Repent from your sins. Repenting is not simply saying "I'm sorry," but literally means "to turn away from." You must turn away from living life your own way and instead trust Jesus to lead you.

Believe that Jesus is the Christ, the son of God.

Accept his gift of forgiveness. He paid it all on the cross. No penance is necessary. No feelings of guilt are required. This is his free gift to you.

Confess your faith in Jesus as your Savior and your Lord. A savior is someone who saves or rescues. A lord is someone who is in charge like a king.

Submit yourself to the lordship of Jesus. Don't just call out to him in times of need, but submit to him and his plan for your life regularly.

Commit to spending time with God every day. Start reading the Bible in the book of John. Take time to listen to what he is saying to you.

WinePressPublishing
Great Books, Defined.

To order additional copies of this book call:
1-877-421-READ (7323)
or please visit our website at
www.WinePressbooks.com

If you enjoyed this quality custom-published book,
drop by our website for more books and information.

www.winepresspublishing.com
"Your partner in custom publishing."

CPSIA information can be obtained at www.ICGtesting.com
Printed in the USA
LVOW040015250212

270315LV00001B/75/P